Photos from Coast to Coast

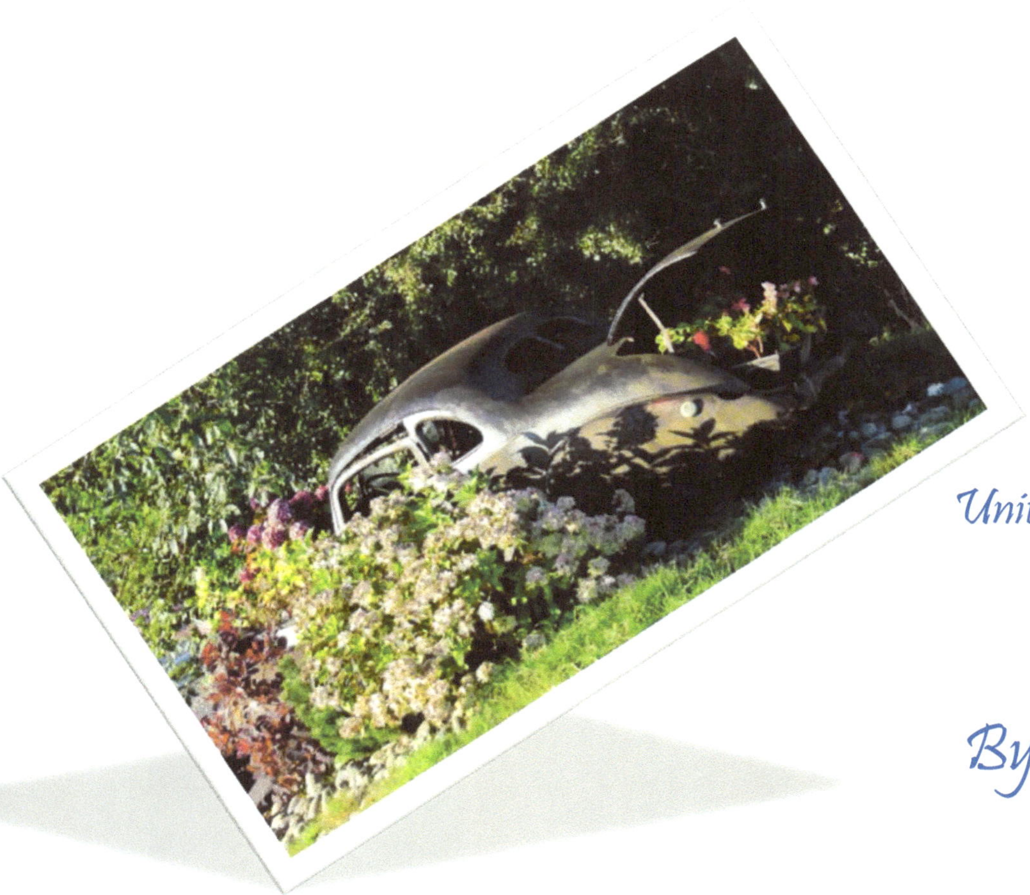

Photographs taken

from across the

United States.

By: Michael Pistner

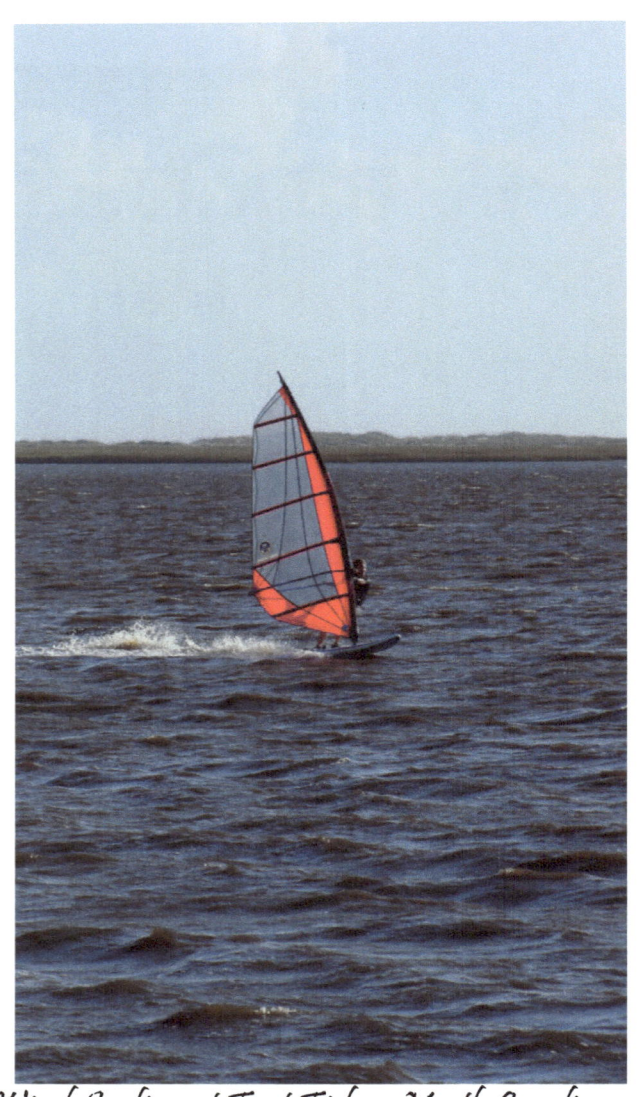

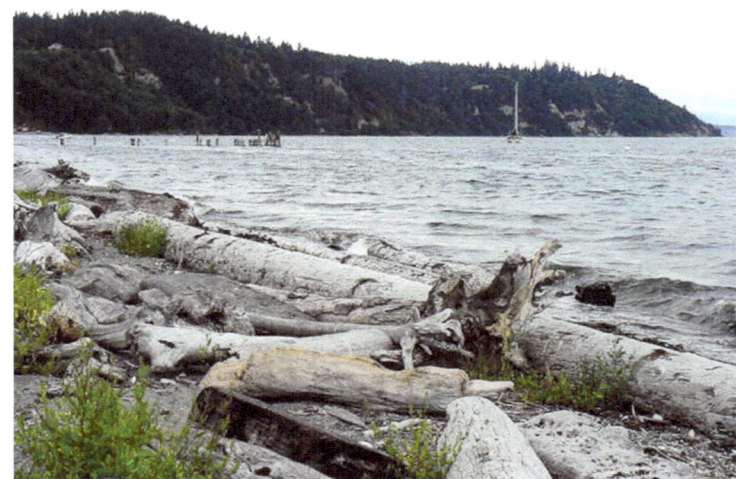

Beach at Whidbey Island, Washington

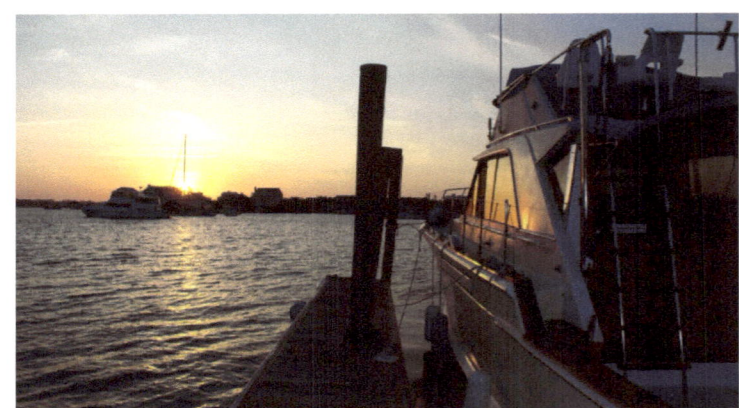

Wind Surfing at Fort Fisher, North Carolina

Boat Docked at Wrightsville Beach, North Carolina

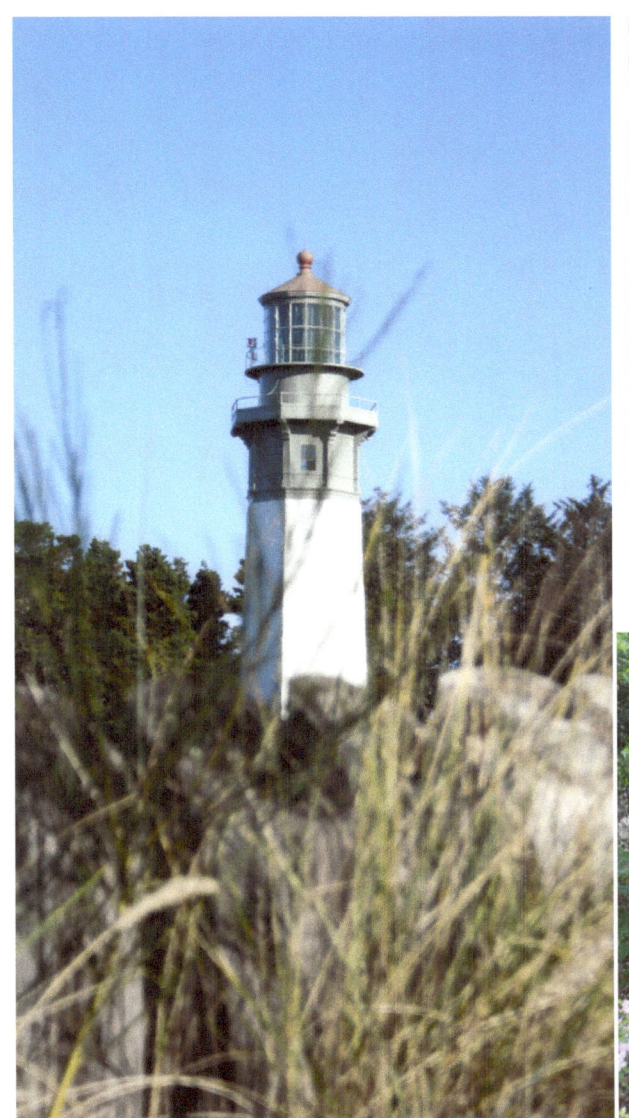

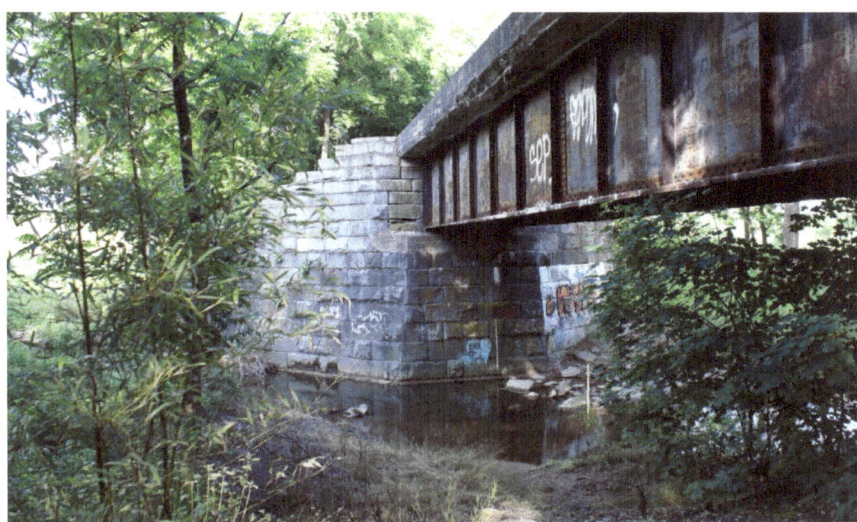

Graffiti On Railroad Trestle

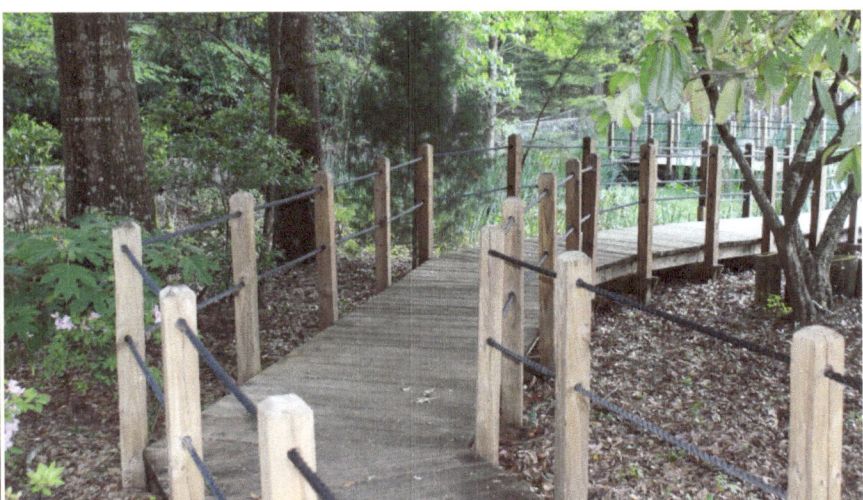

Light House at West Port, Washington

Wooden Path at Arlie Gardens in Wilmington, NC

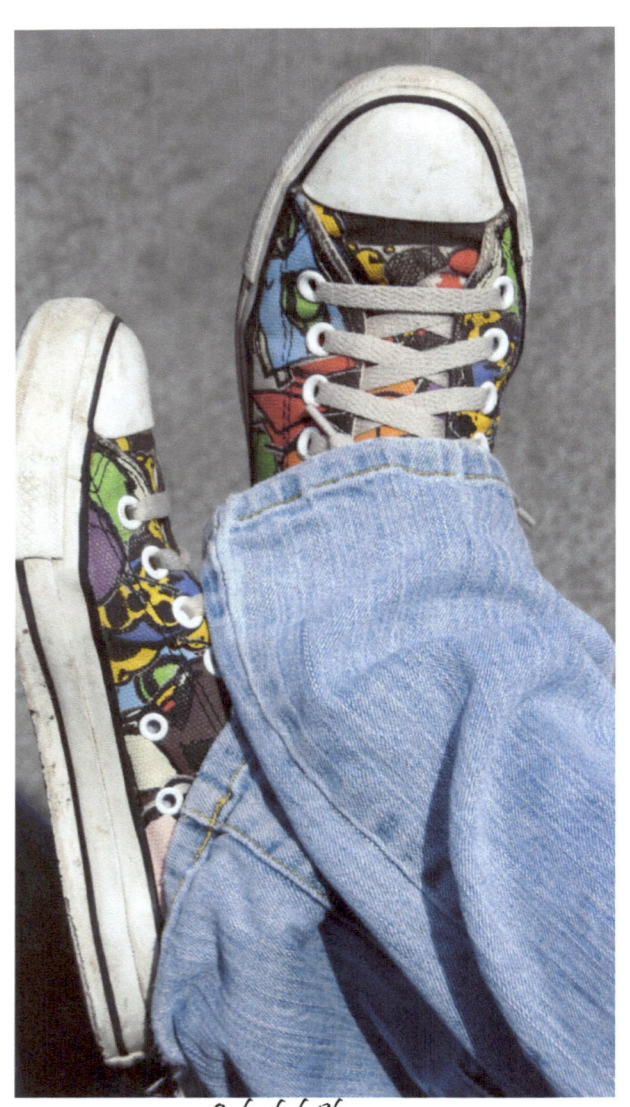

Colorful Shoes

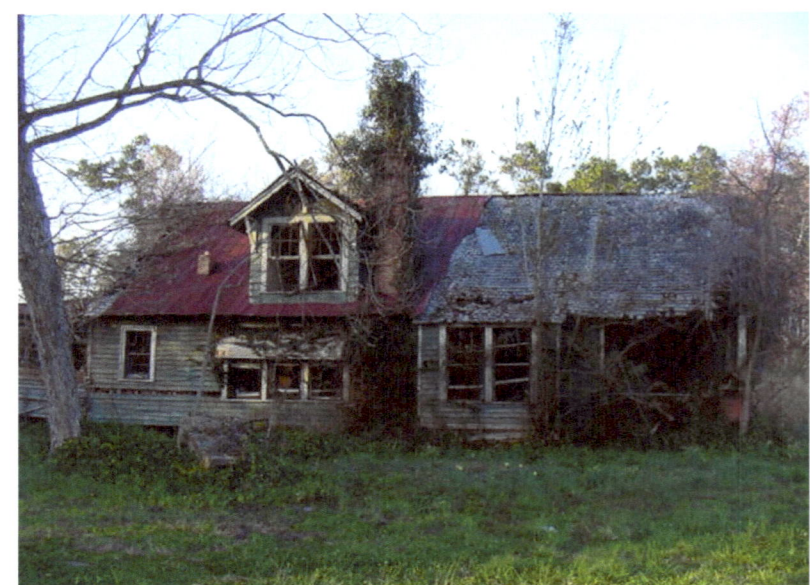

Old House in Teachey, North Carolina

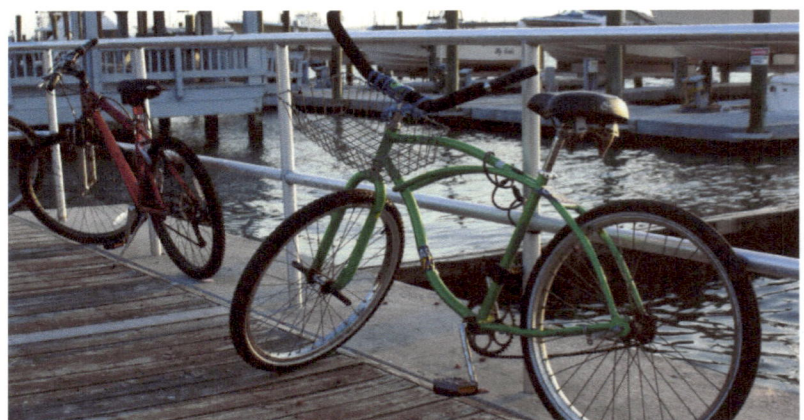

Bicycles at the Beach, Wrightsville Beach, NC

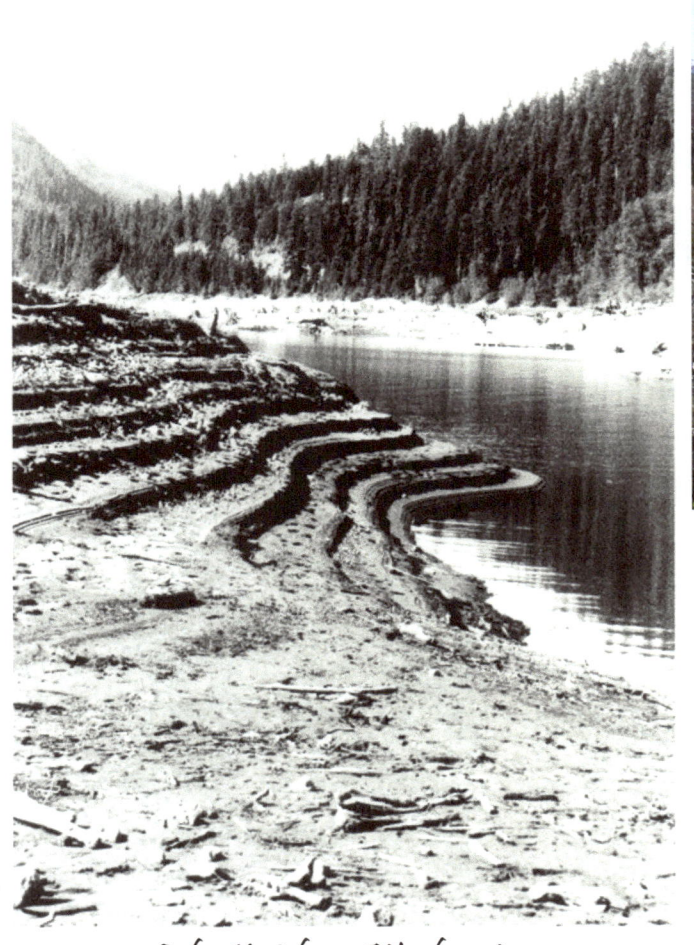

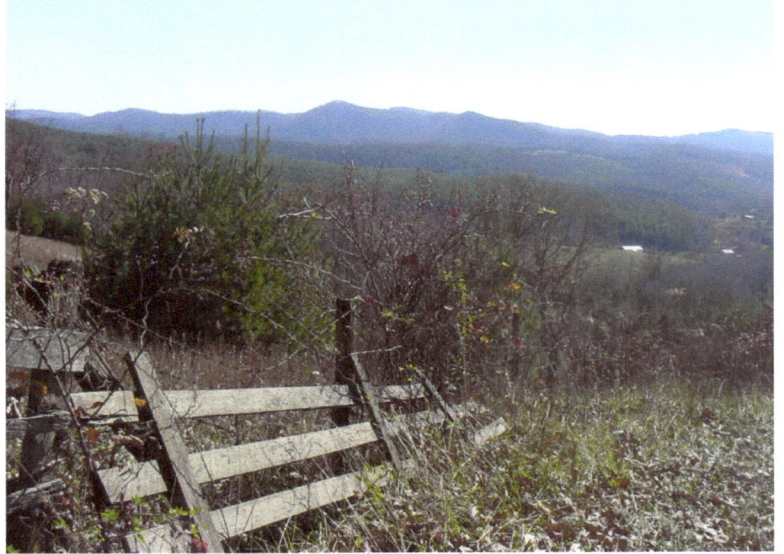

Broken Fence Blue Ridge Mountains

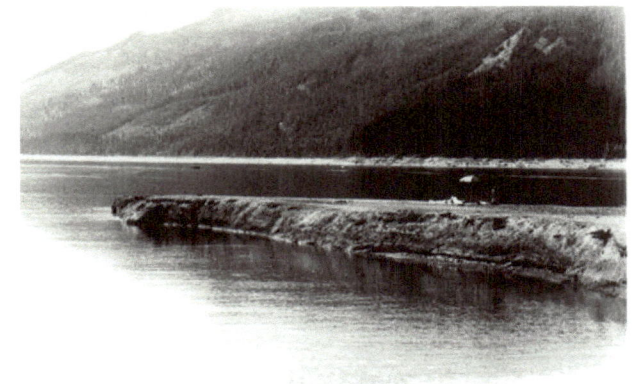

Lake Katchess, Washington

Another Black & White at Katchess

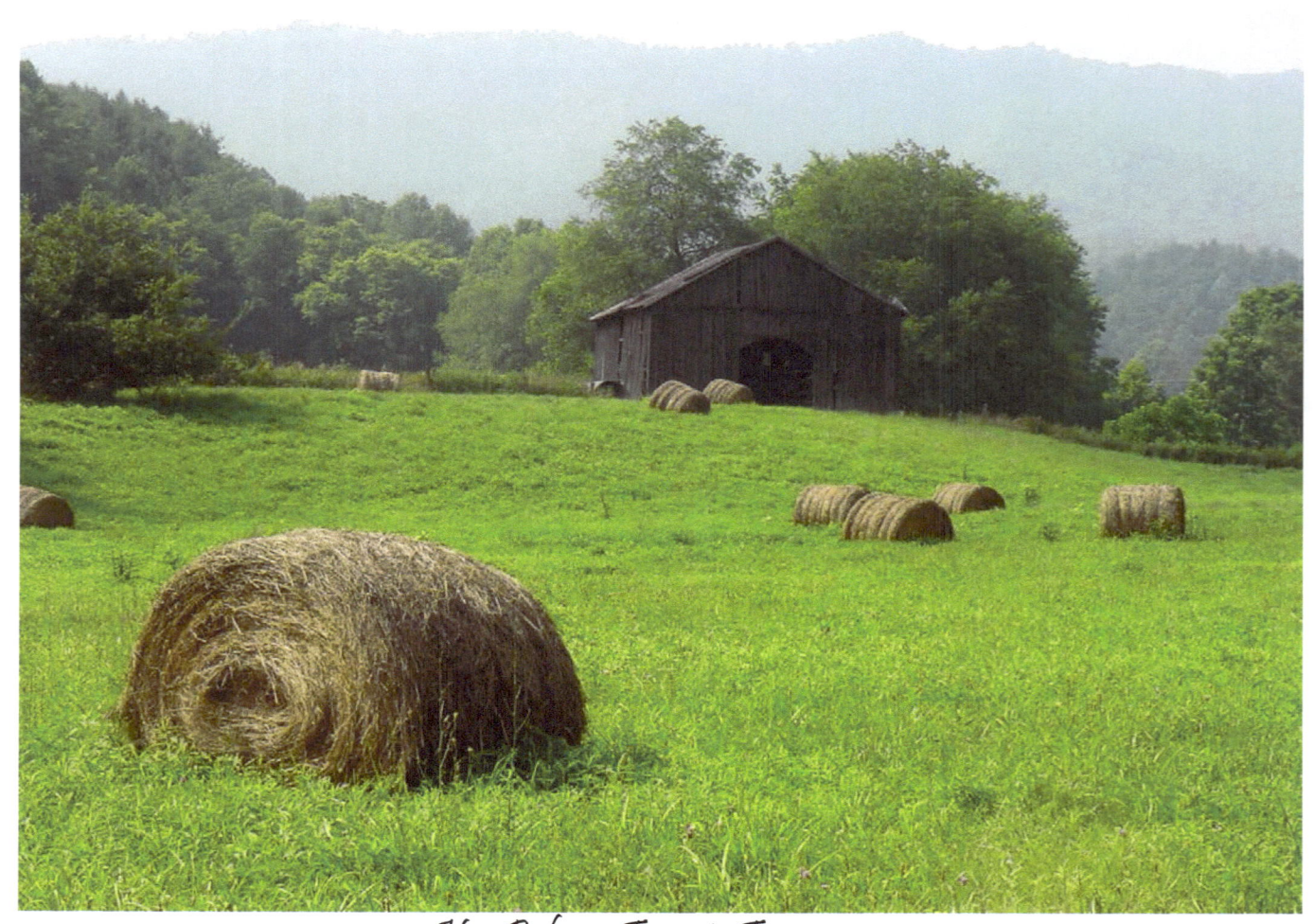

Hay Bales on Farm in Tennessee

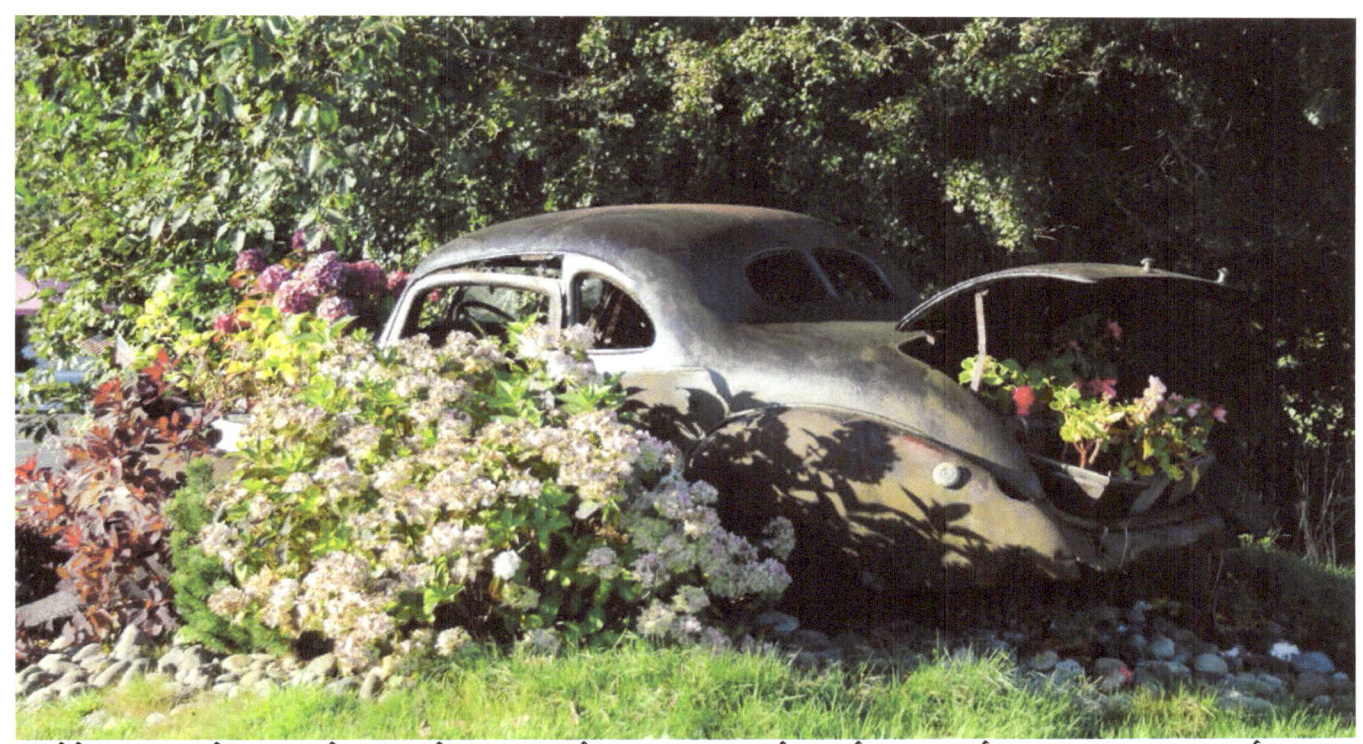

Old Car Used in Landscape where it Broke Down, Used as Flower Bed ~ West Port, Washington

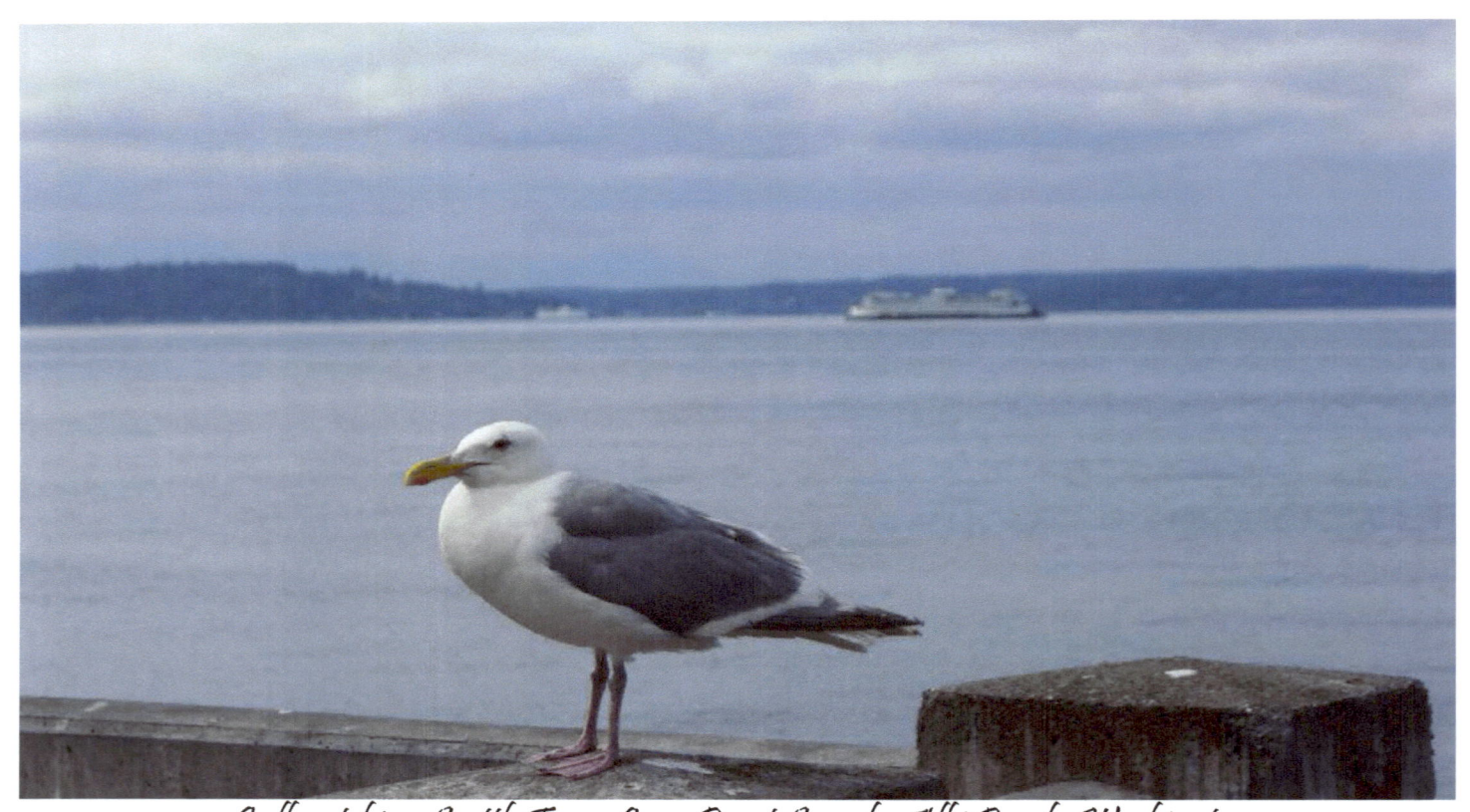

Gull watching Seattle Ferry Cross Puget Sound – Alki Beach, Washington

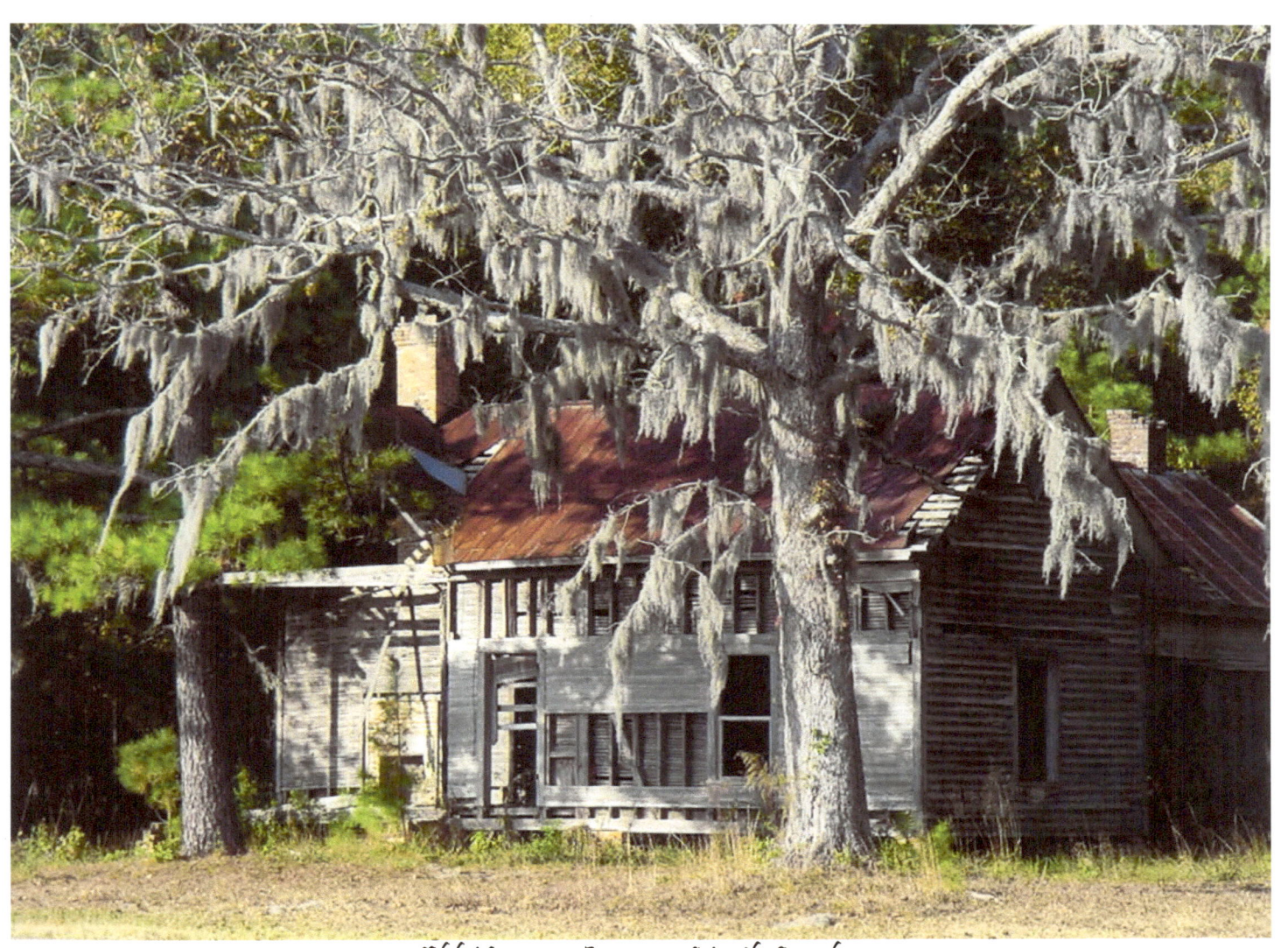

Old House in Burgaw, North Carolina

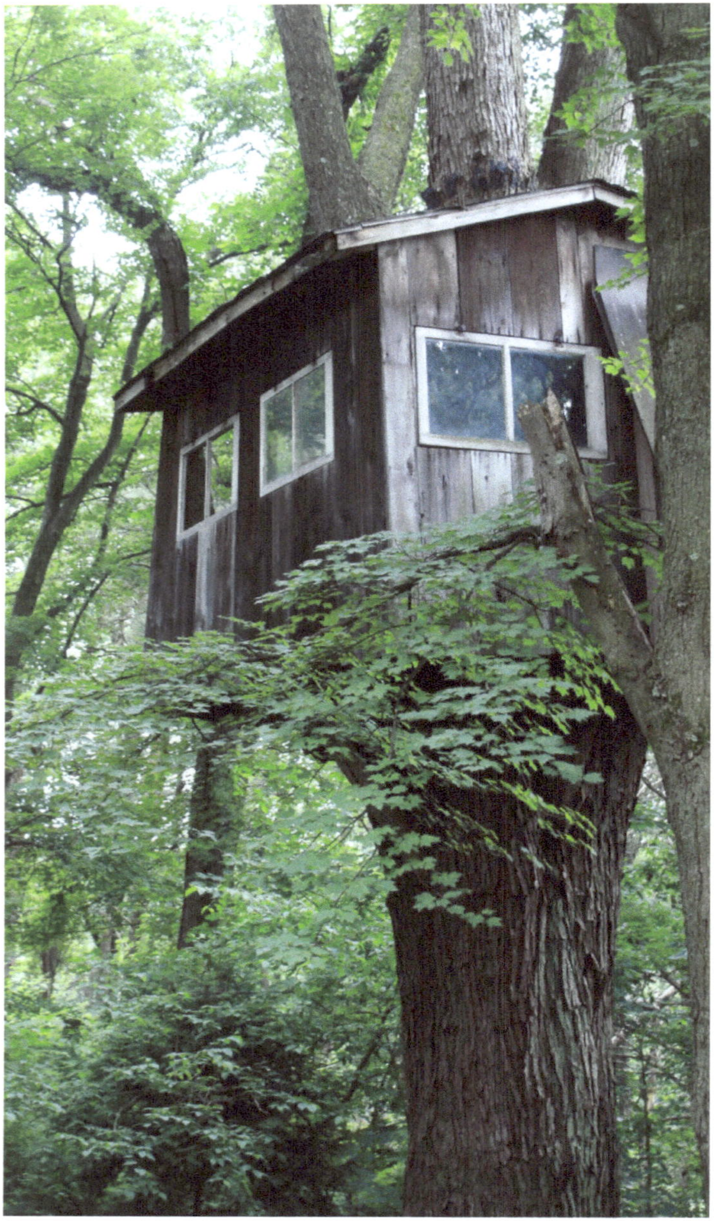

True Meaning of Tree House – Pennsylvania

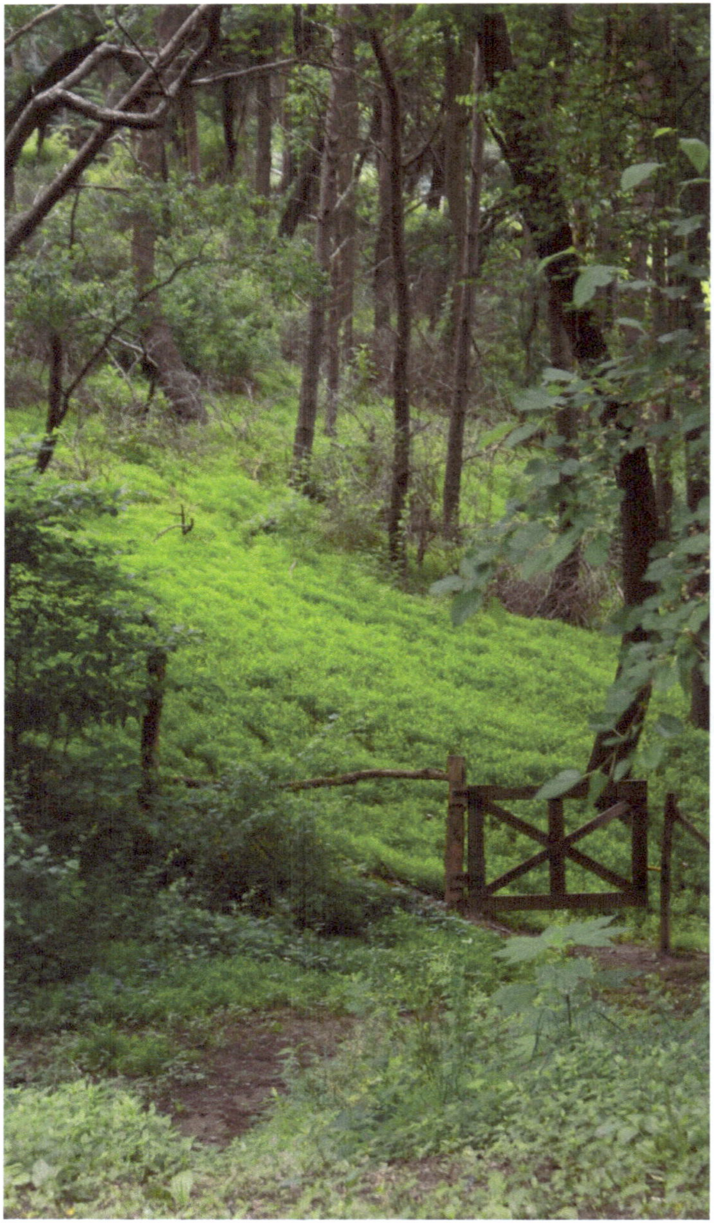

Farm gate in Lush Field – Pennsylvania

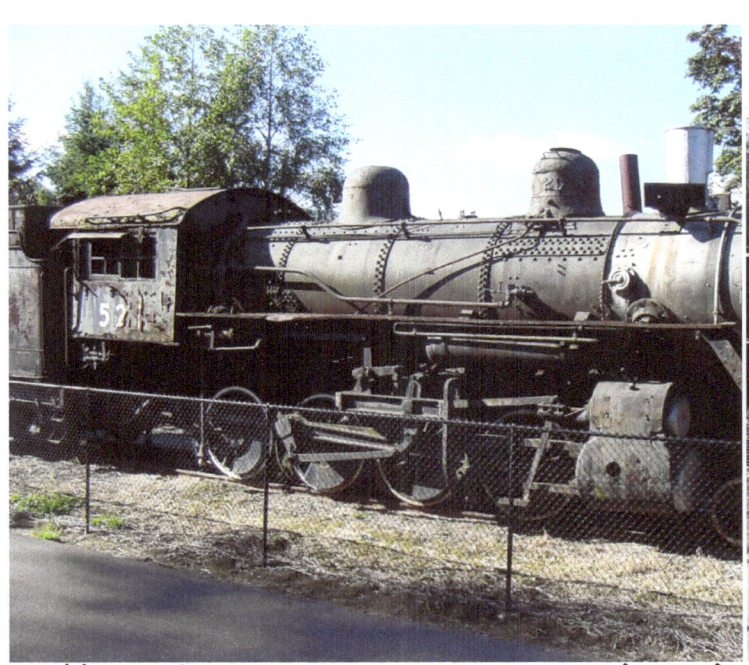

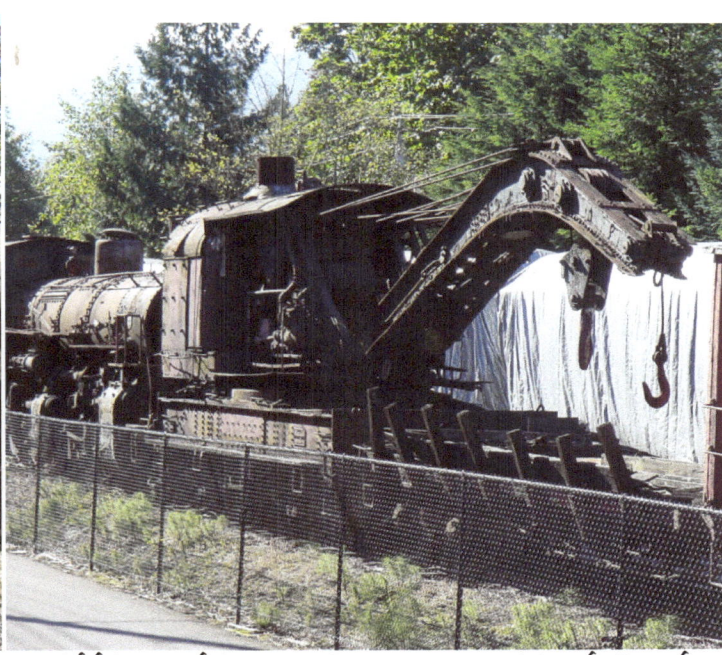

Old, Out of Service Logging Engine – North Bend, Washington

Old Rusted Logging Equipment – North Bend, Washington

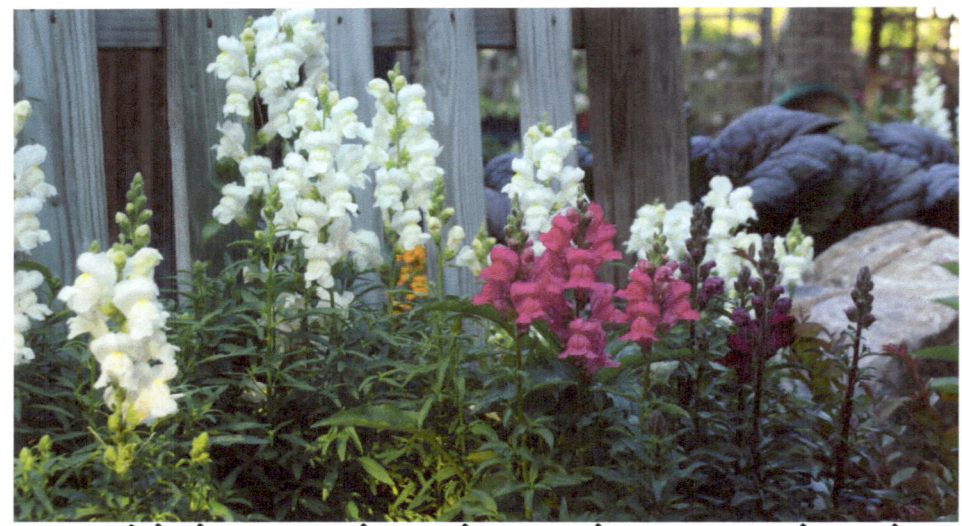

Beautiful Flowers at Arlie Gardens – Wilmington, North Carolina

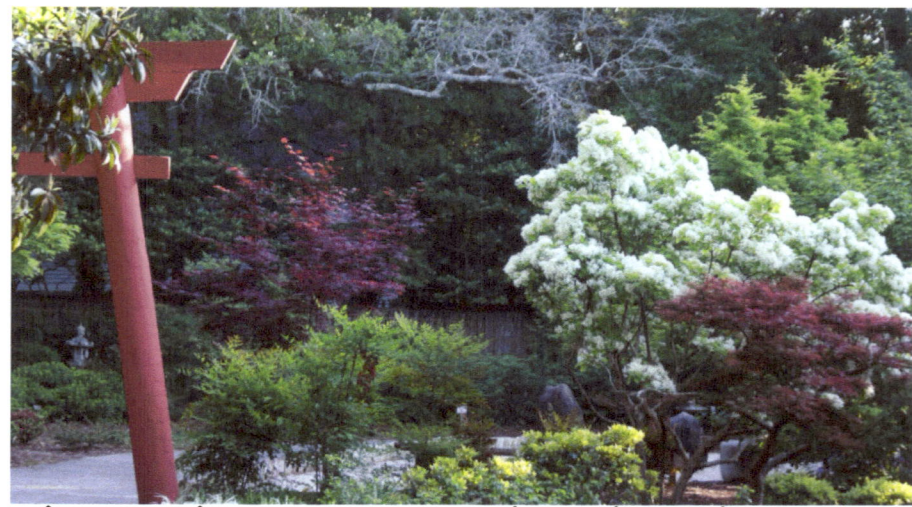

Chinese Garden Arrangement at Arlie Gardens Wilmington, NC

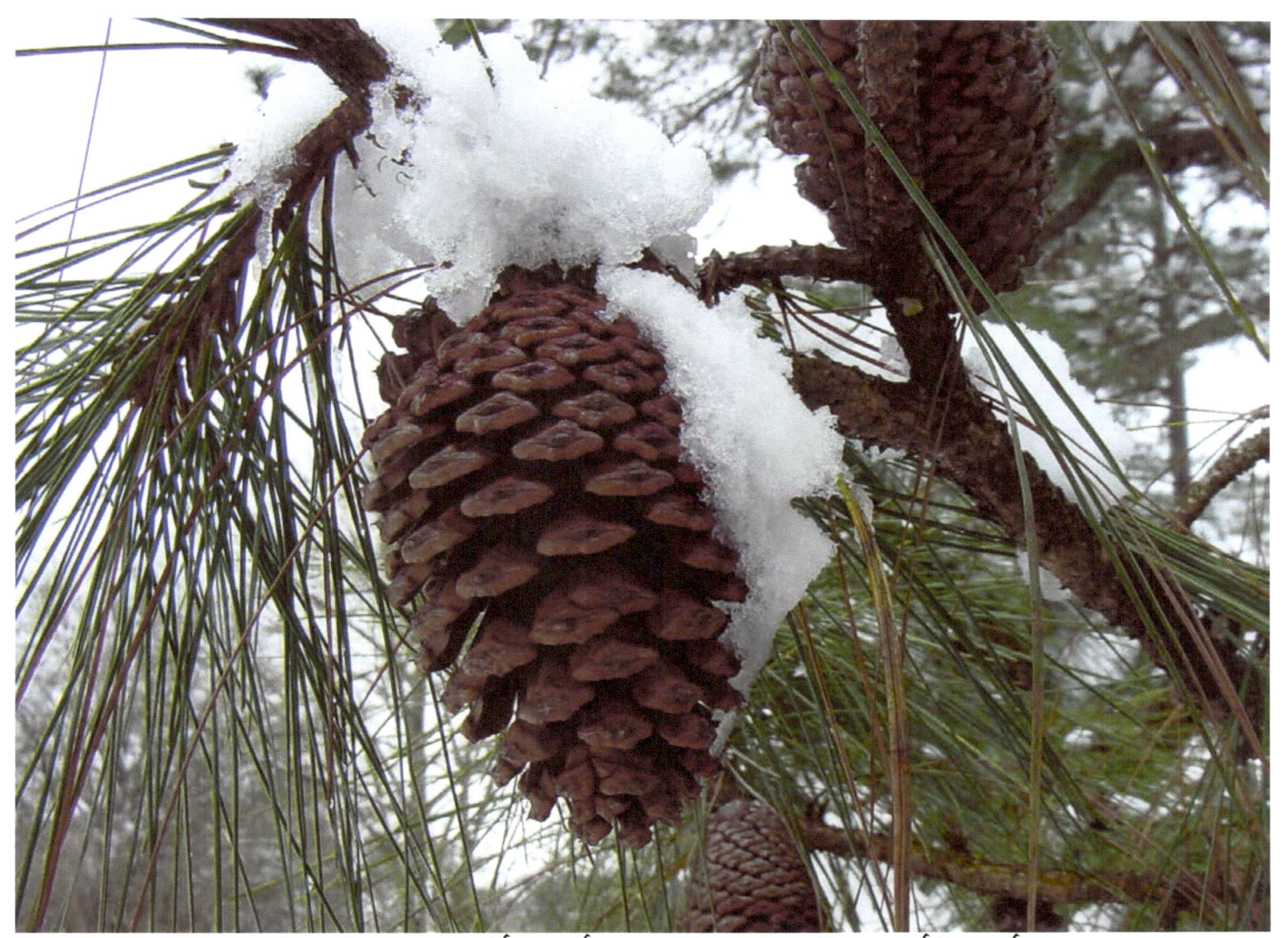

Rare Snow in North Carolina covering a Pine Cone and Branch

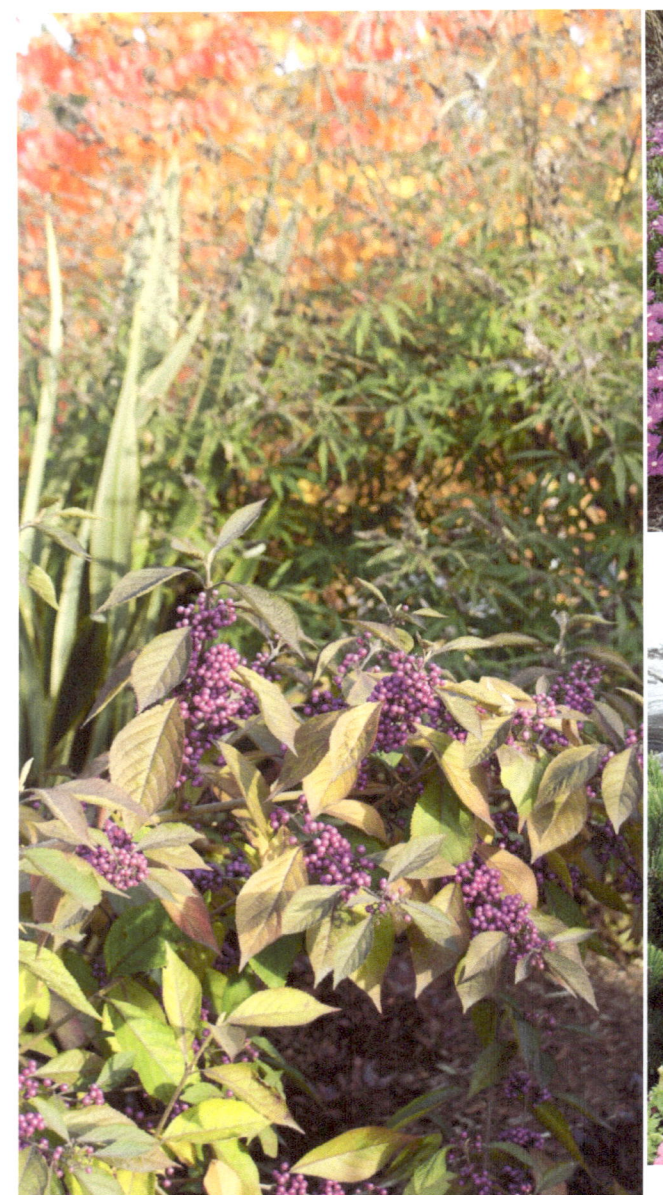

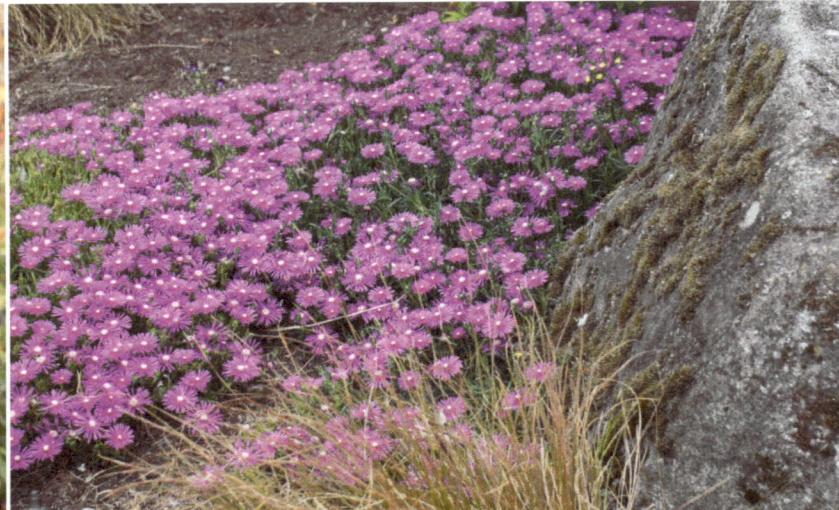

Flowered Landscape – Alki Beach, Washington

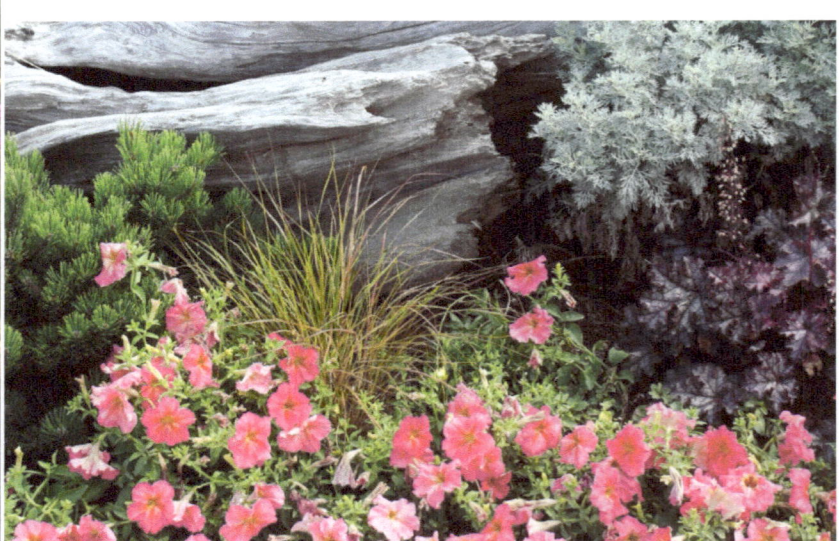

Flowers with Driftwood at Alki Beach

Fall Flowers in Fall City, Washington

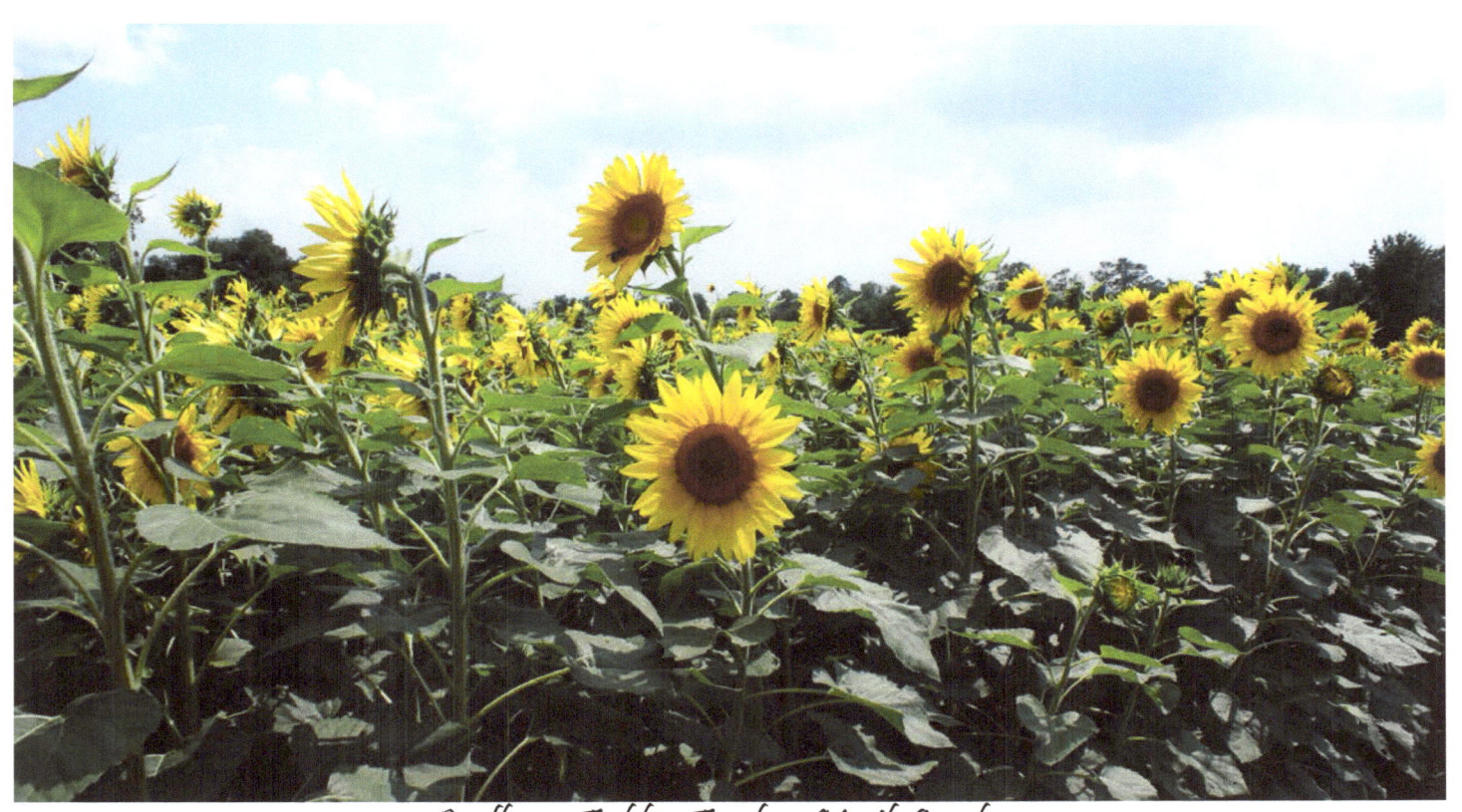

Sunflower Field in Teachey, North Carolina

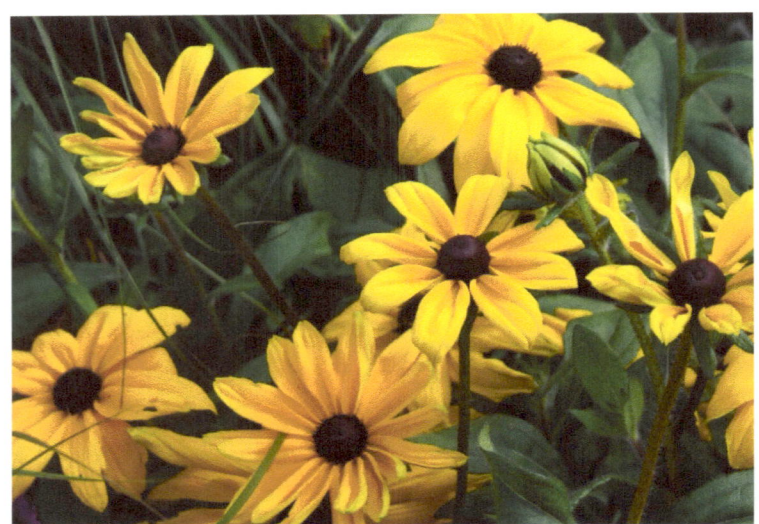

Brown Eyed Susans

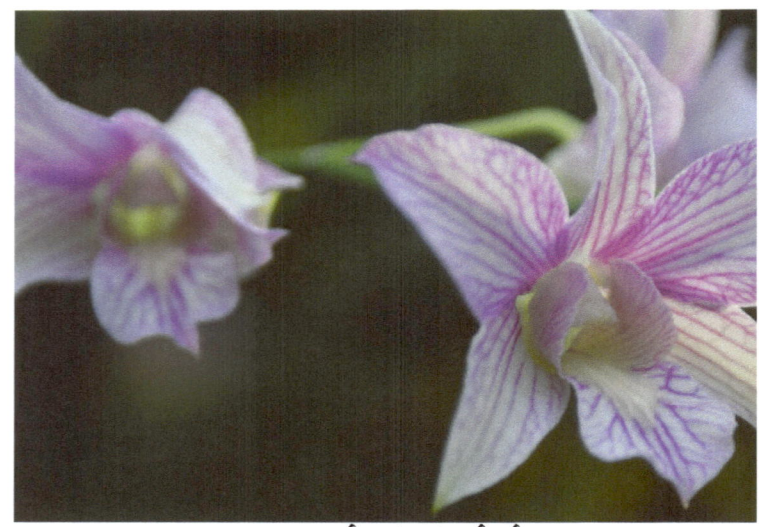

Grandma's Orchid

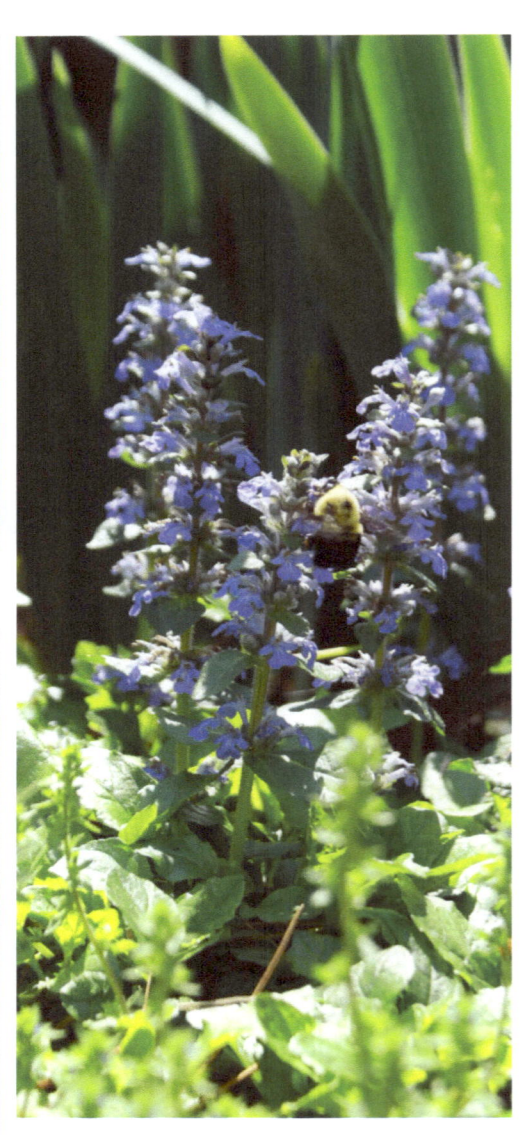

Bumble Bee Collecting Pollen

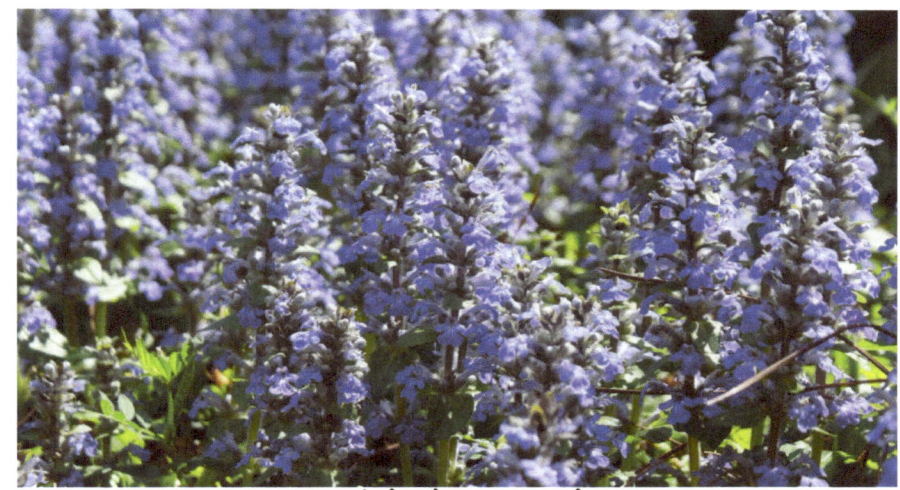

Beautiful Blue Ground Cover

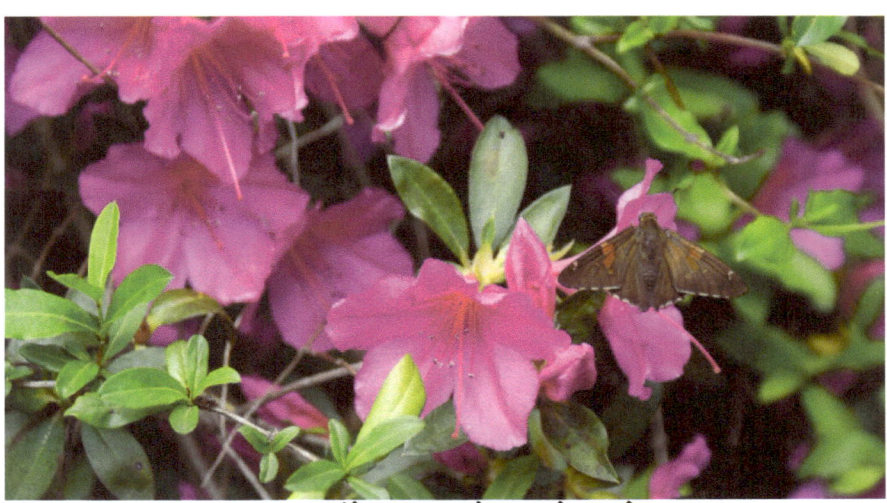

Butterfly on Pink Azalea Plant

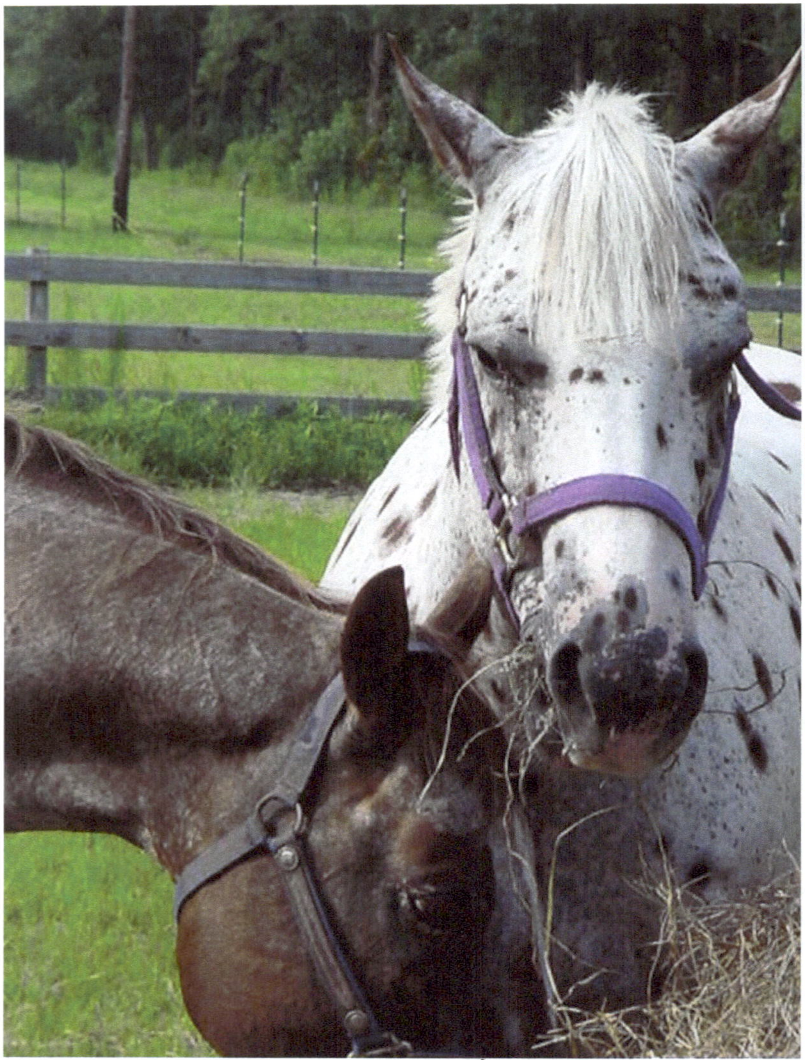

Eating Together

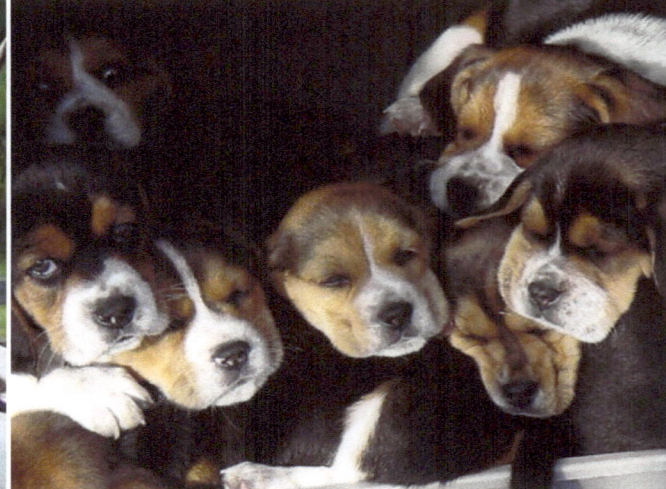

Beagle Pups

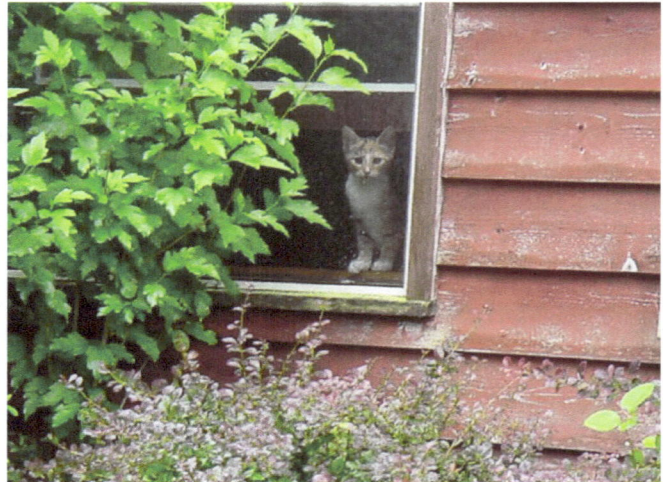

Cat In Window

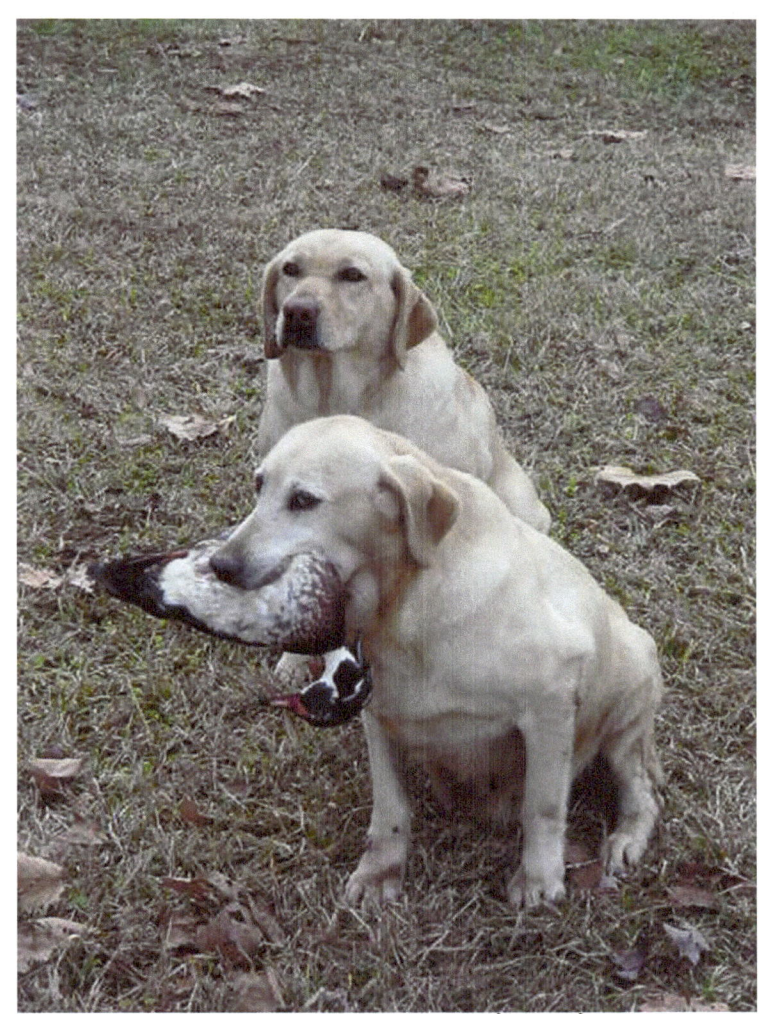

Pair Of Retrievers with Duck

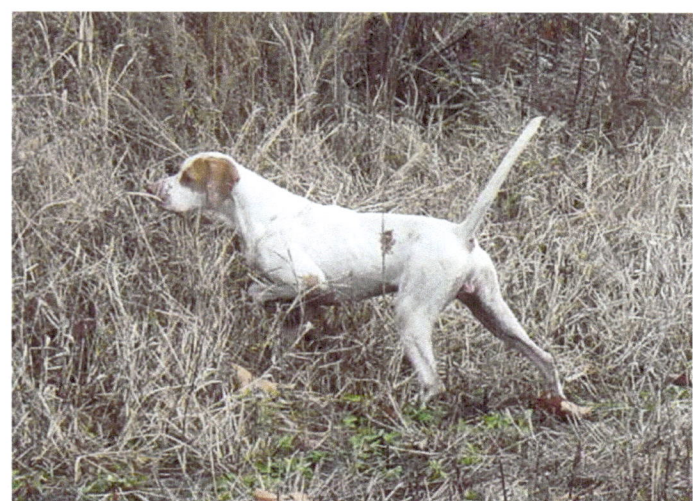

Perfect Point

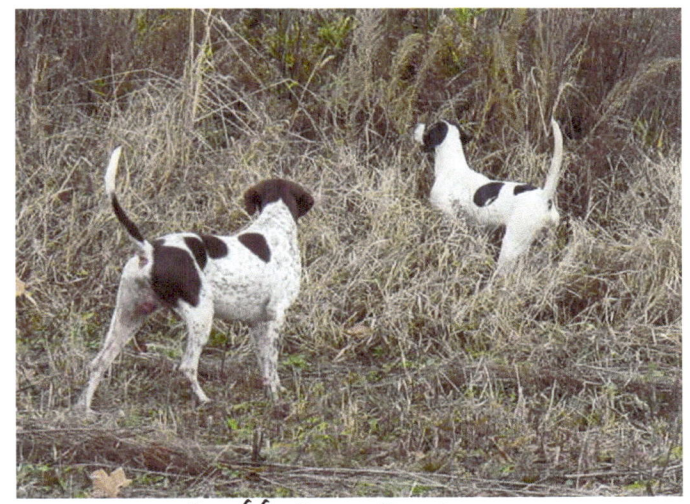

Double Team Pointers

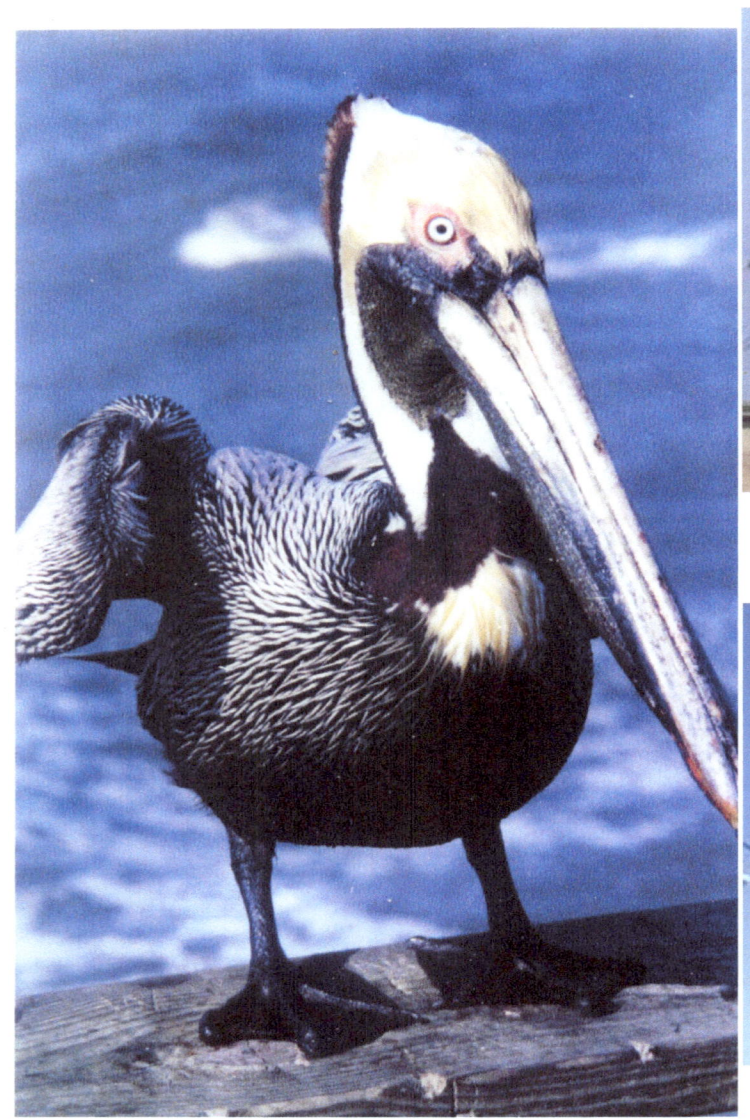

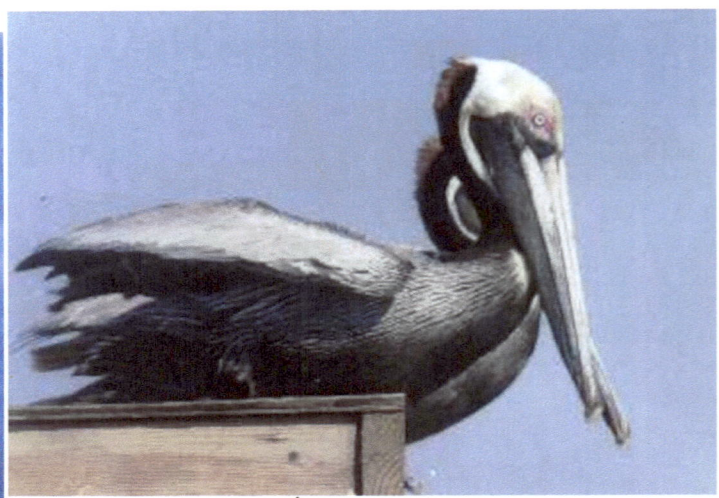

Pelicans On Pier

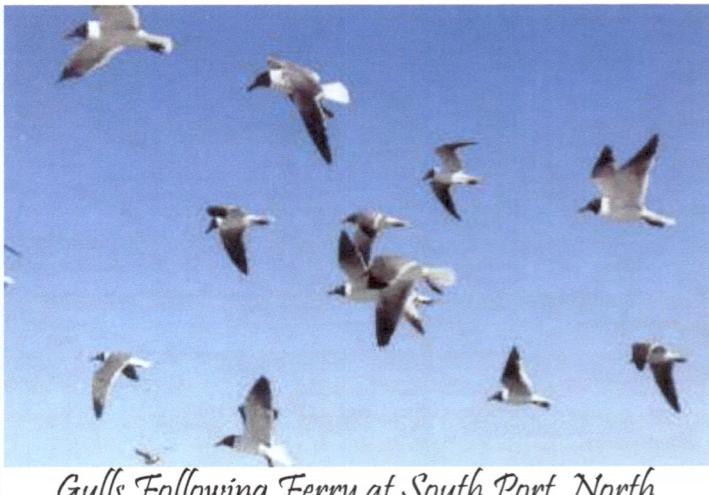

Pelican At Kure Beach, North Carolina

Gulls Following Ferry at South Port, North Carolina

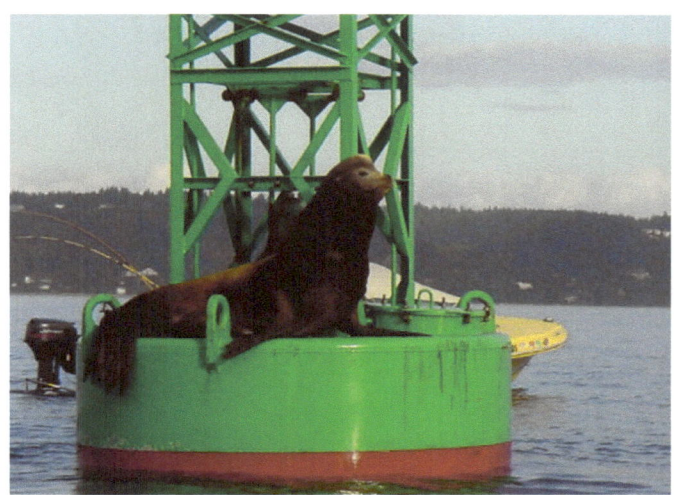

Seal In Puget Sound ~ Washington

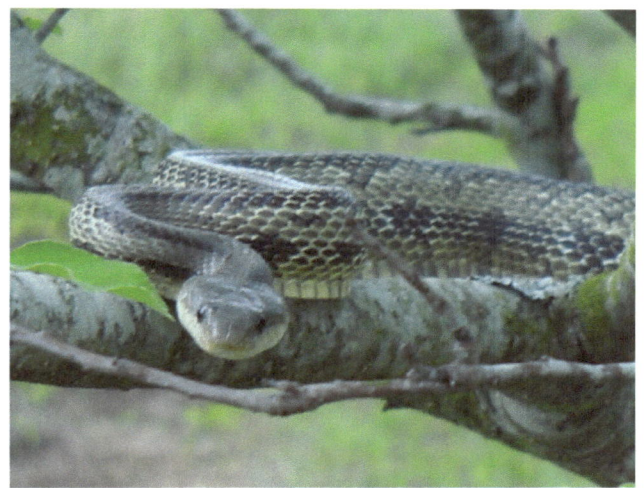

Snake In A Tree

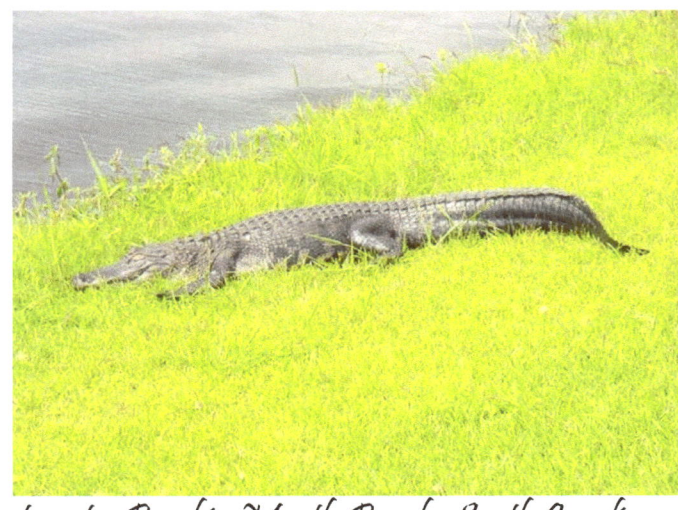

Alligator at a Pond in Myrtle Beach, South Carolina

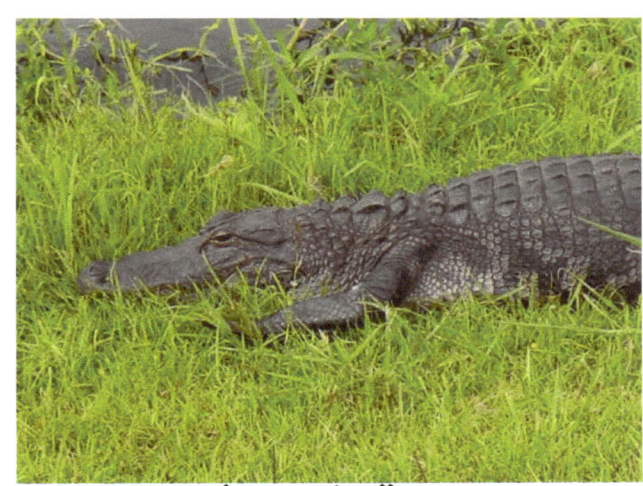

Close up of Alligator

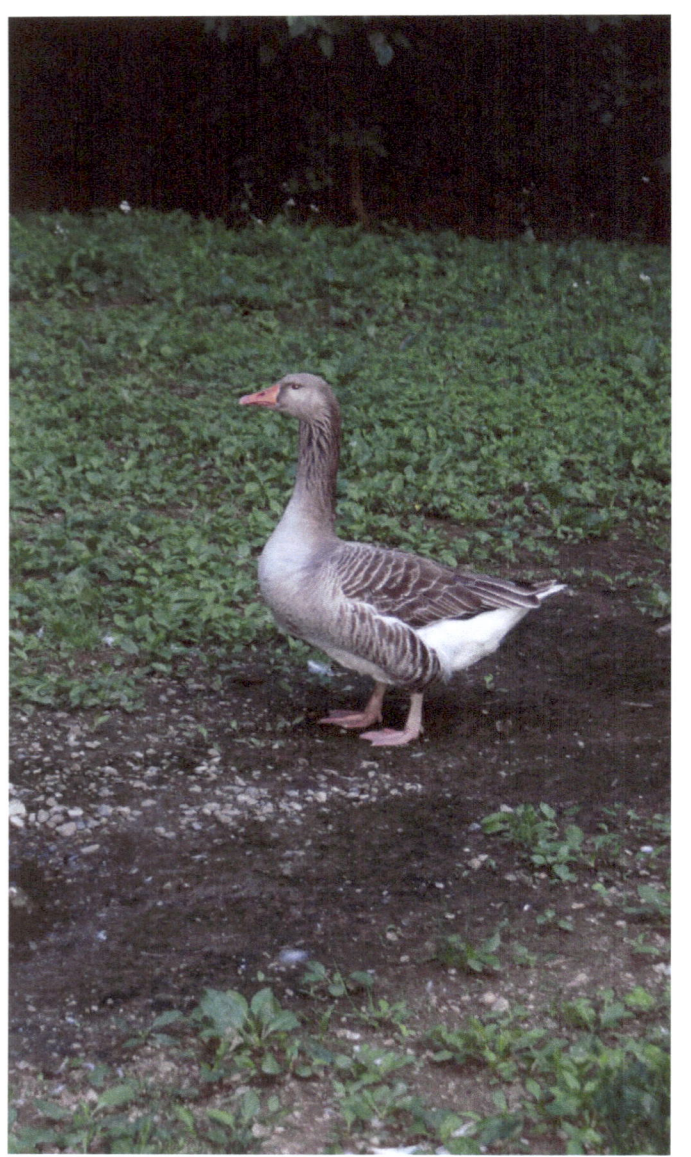

Goose!

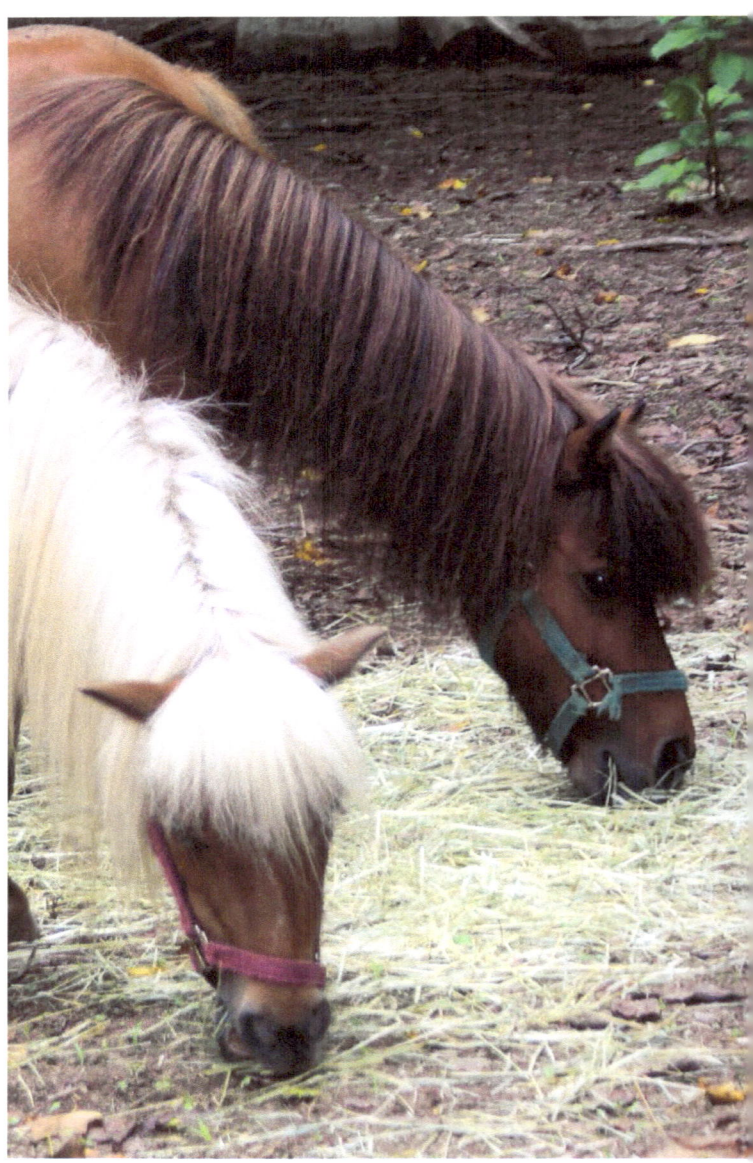

Minies

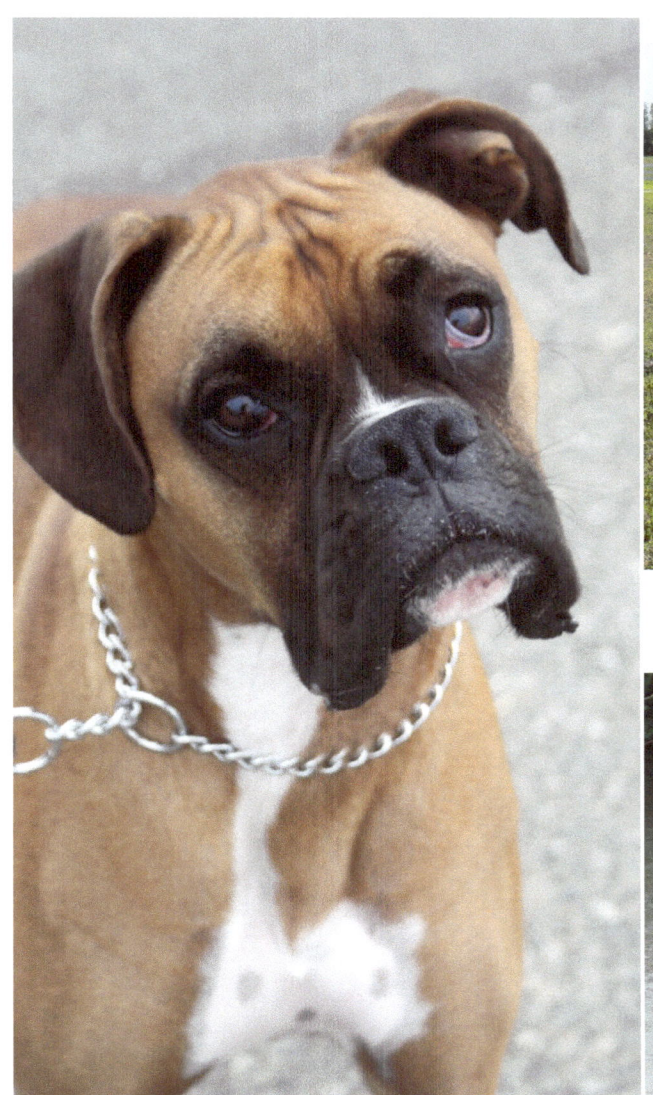

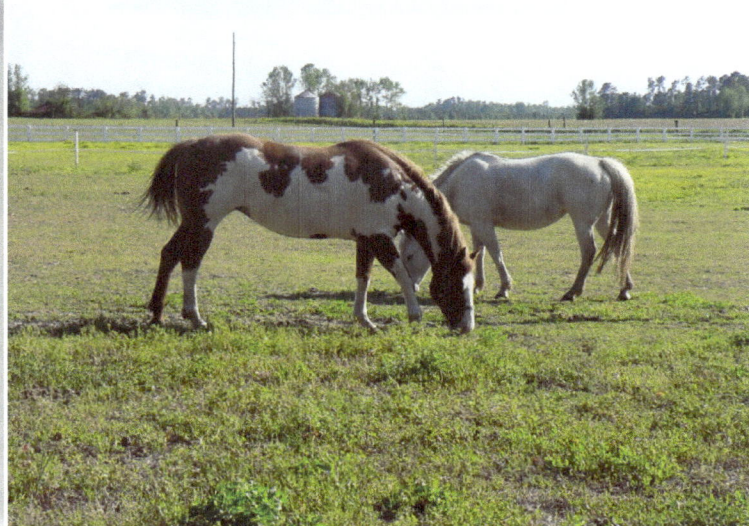

Horses In a Field

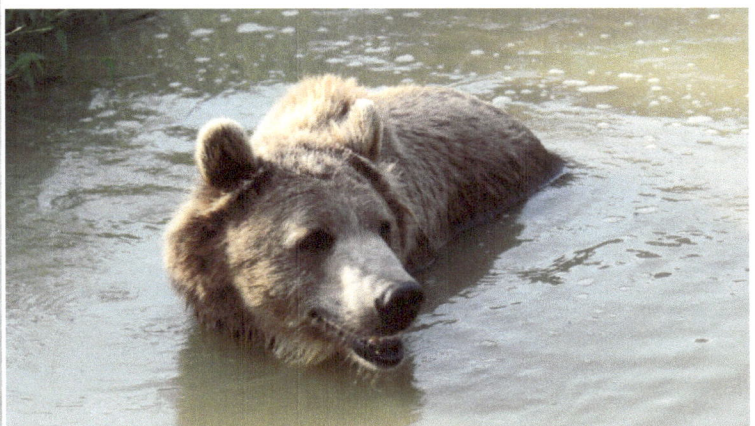

Bear In Pond

Boxer at Alki Beach, Washington

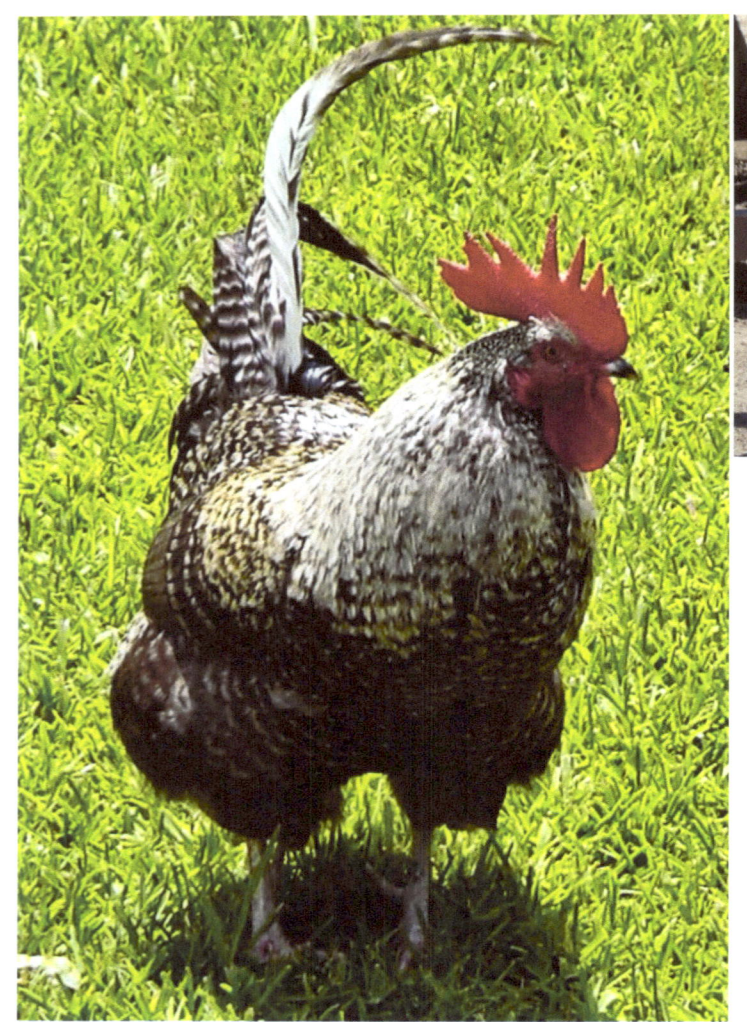

King Of The Roosters

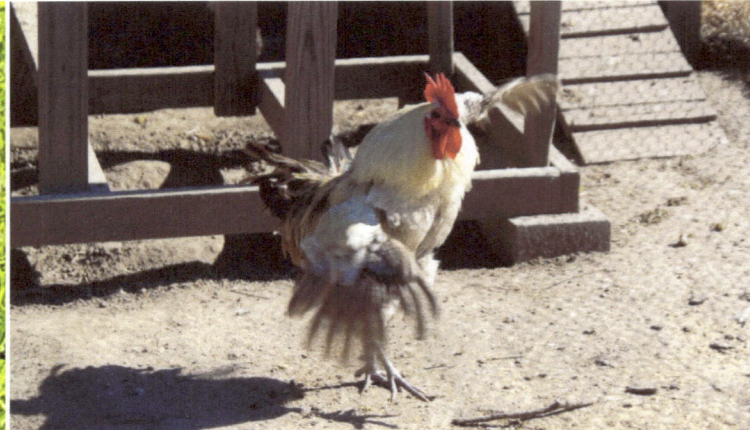

Rooster Showing Off

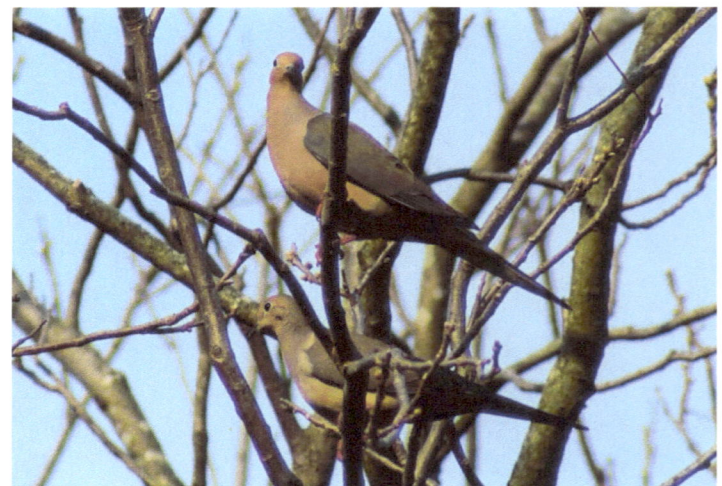

Pair Of Doves In A Tree

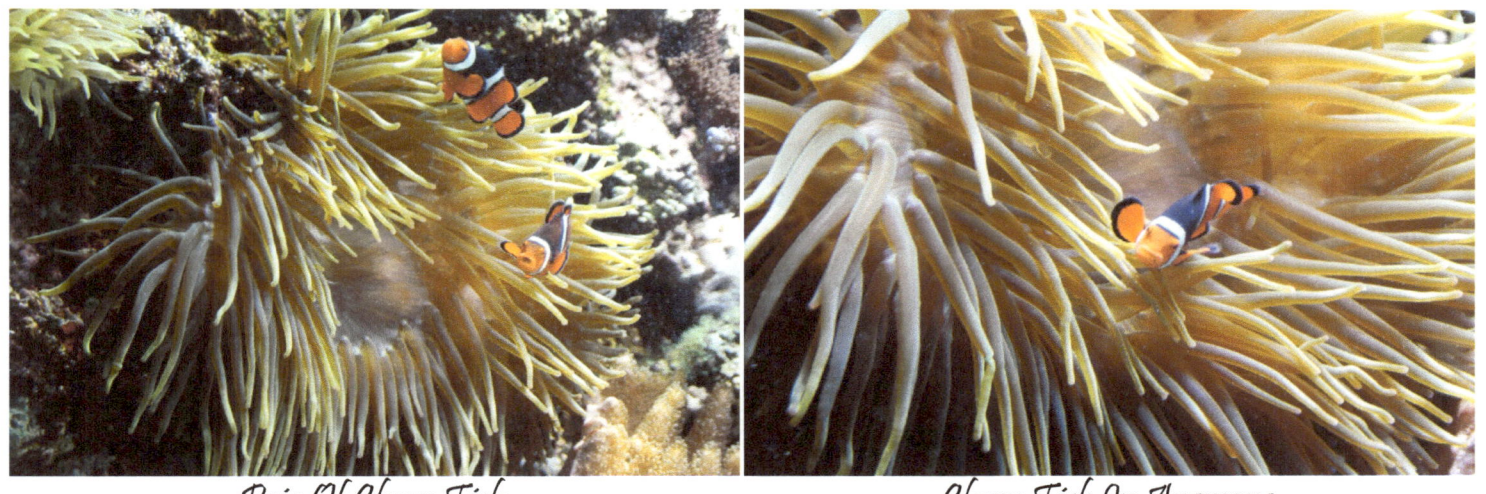

Pair Of Clown Fish   *Clown Fish In Anemone*

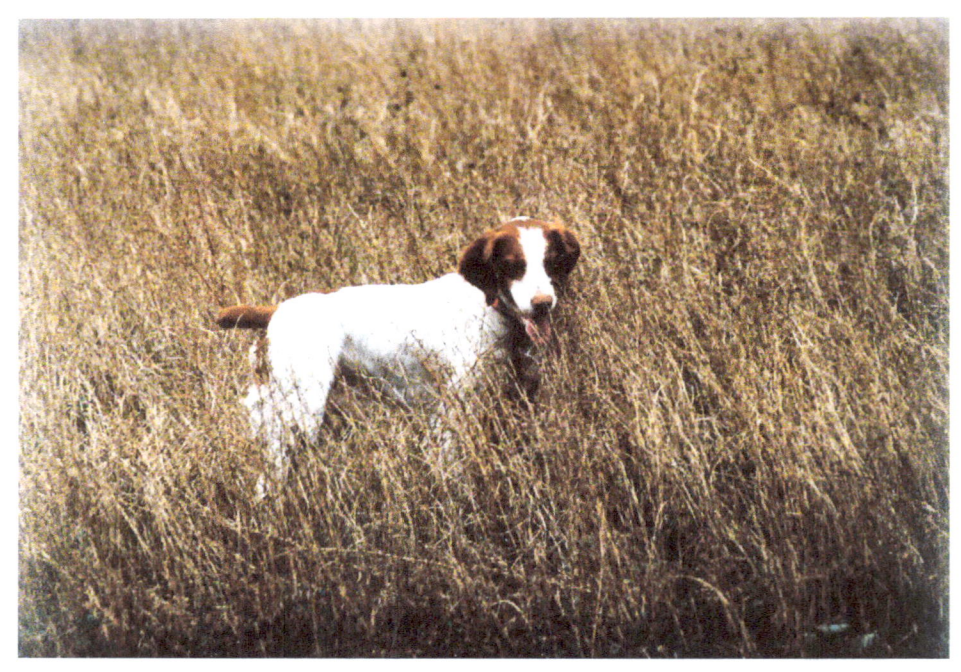

A Friends Champion Brittany Spaniel On the Job

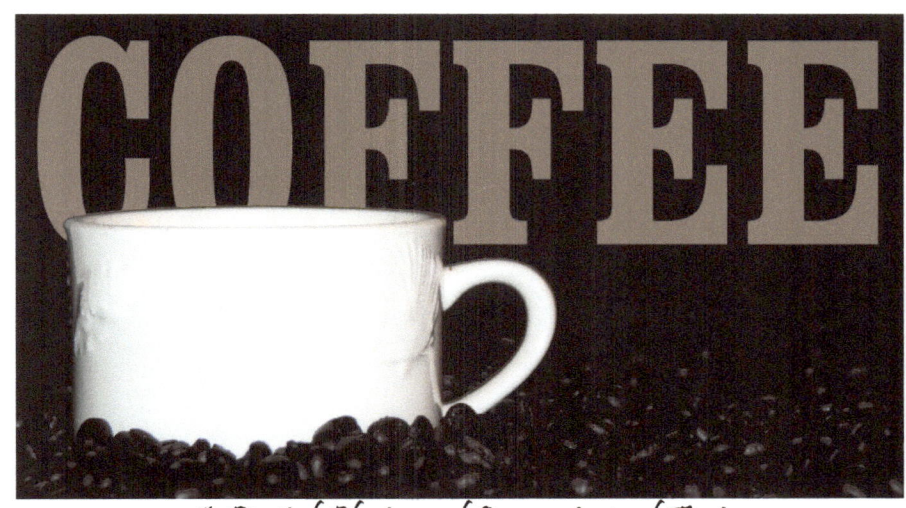

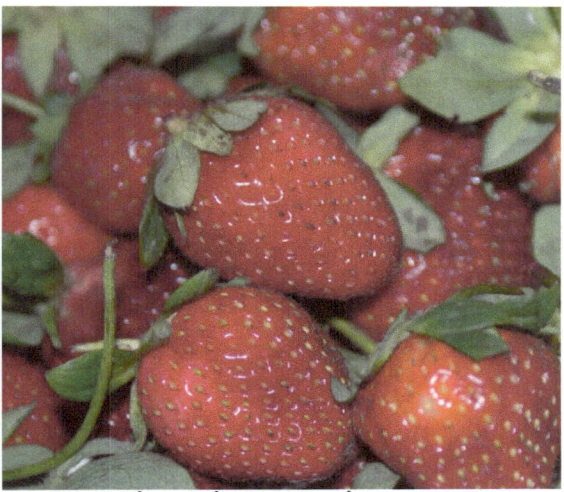

A Digital Photo and Computerized Text

Fresh Red, Ripe, Plump, Juicy
Strawberries

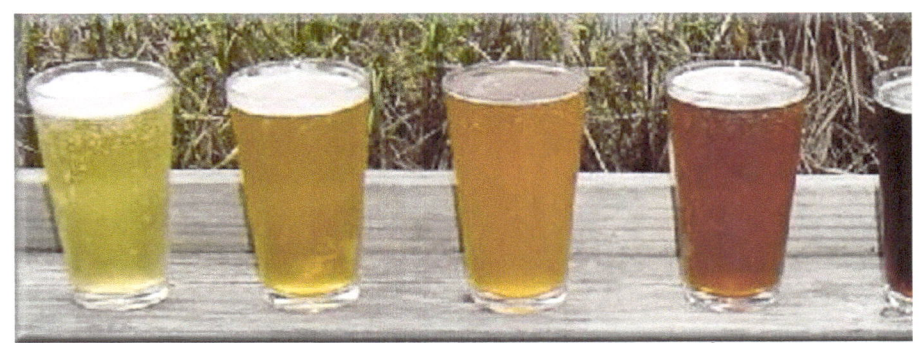

A Wide Selection of Micro Brewed Beers In Myrtle Beach, South Carolina

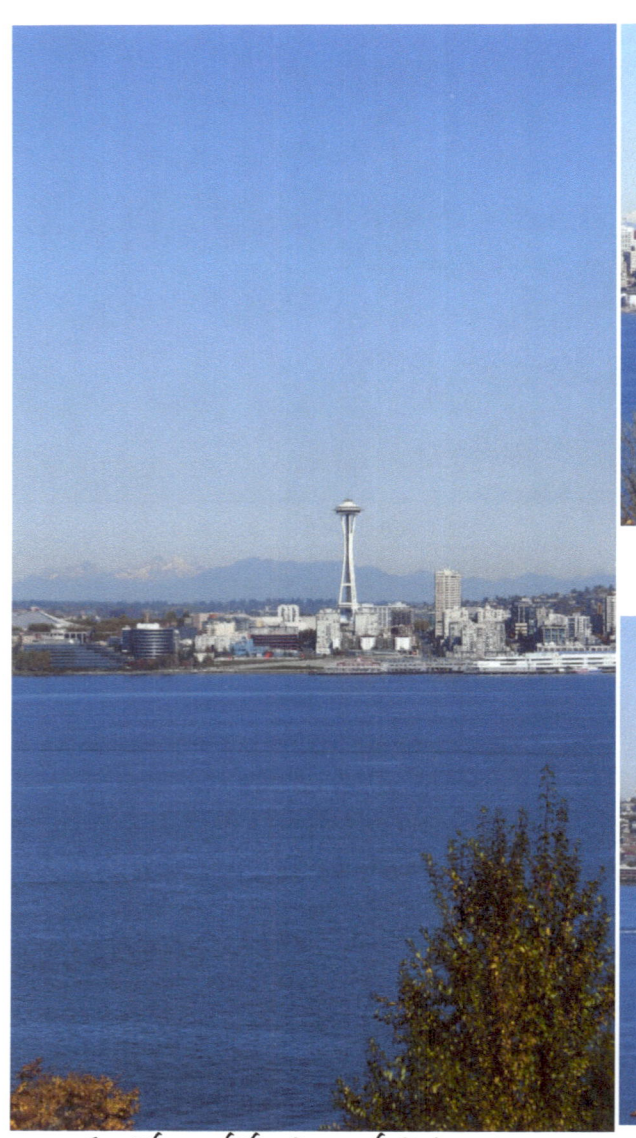

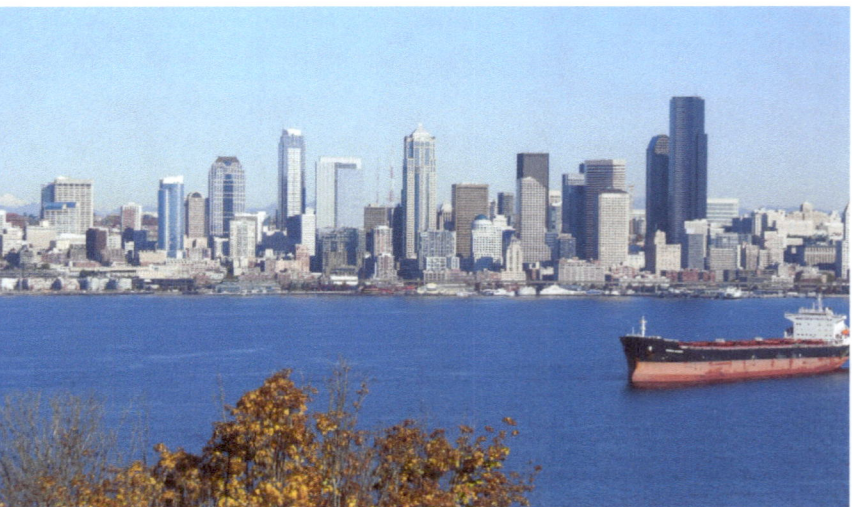

Seattle Skyline With Tanker in Puget Sound

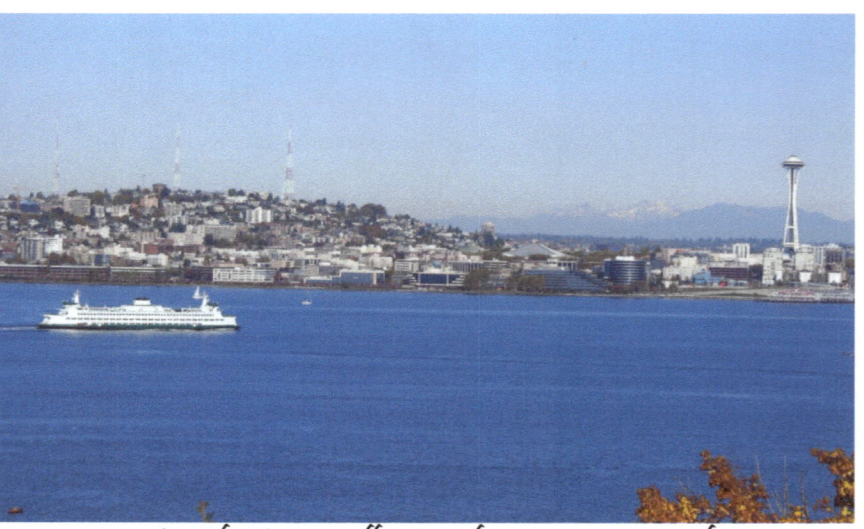

Seattle and the Cascade Mountains

Seattle From Alki Beach Ferry in Sound

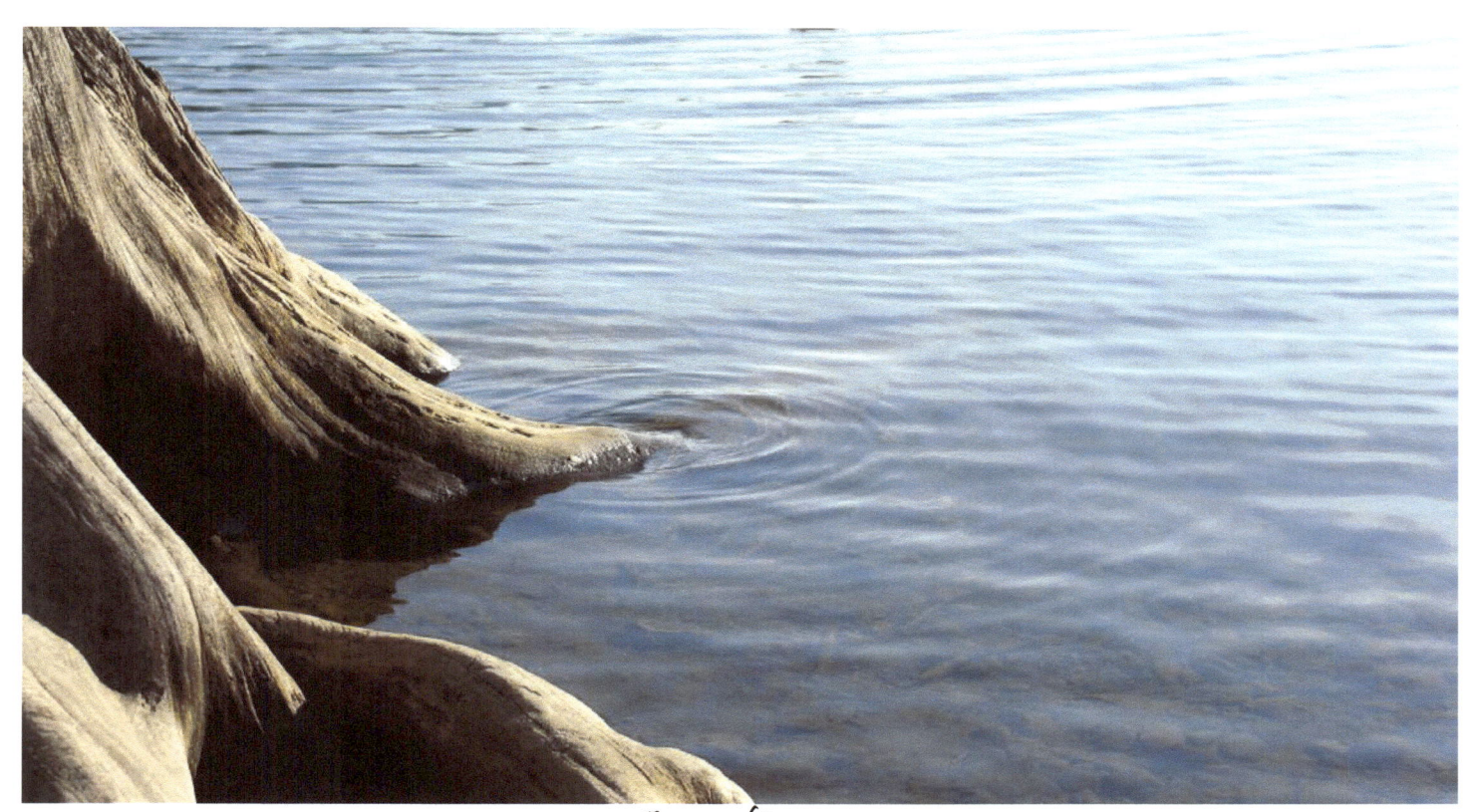

Tranquility…

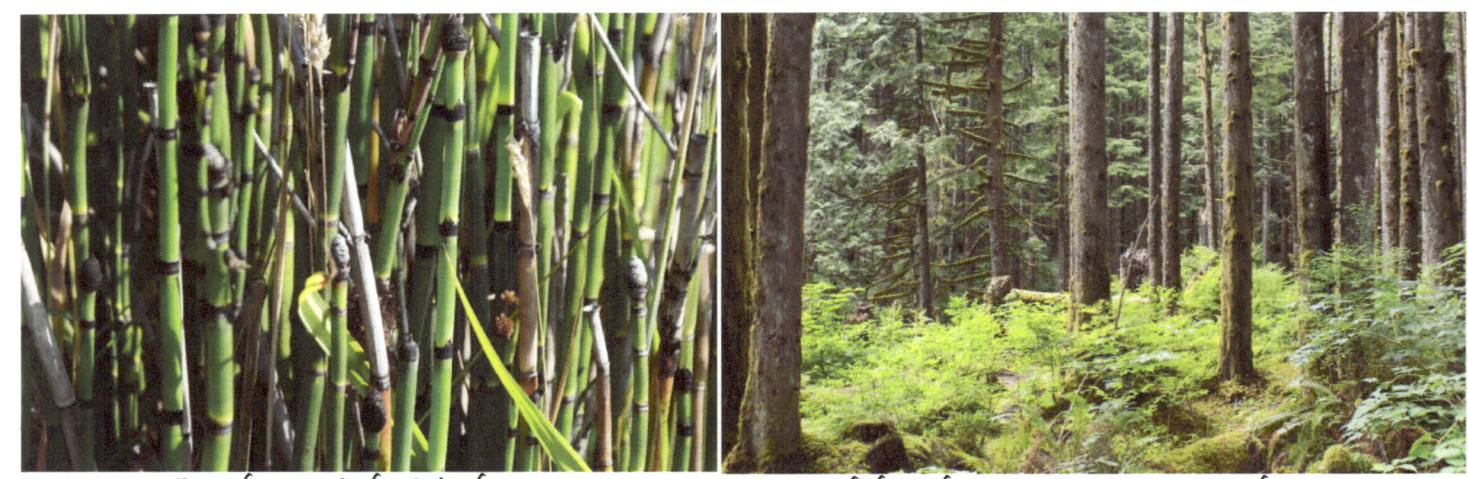

Bamboo in Lake Washington

Beautiful Lush Green Forrest – Washington State

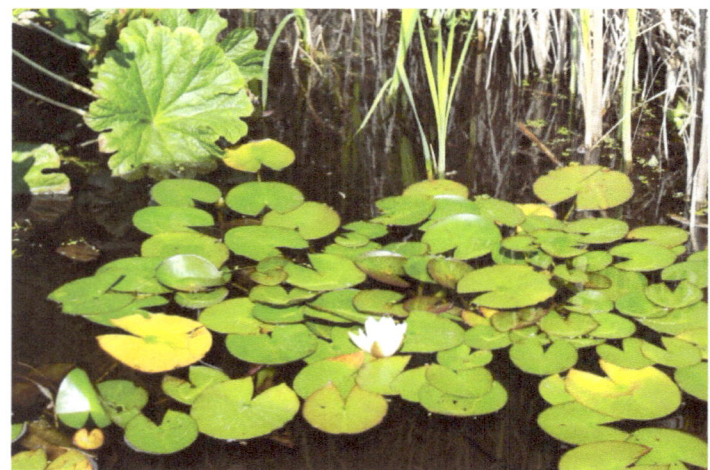

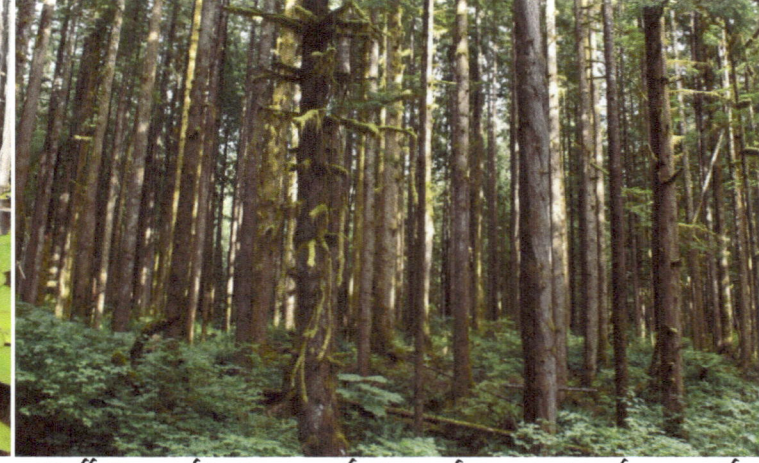

Bamboo & Lilly Pads on the Edge of the Lake

Tall Straight Trees with Lots of Green Undergrowth

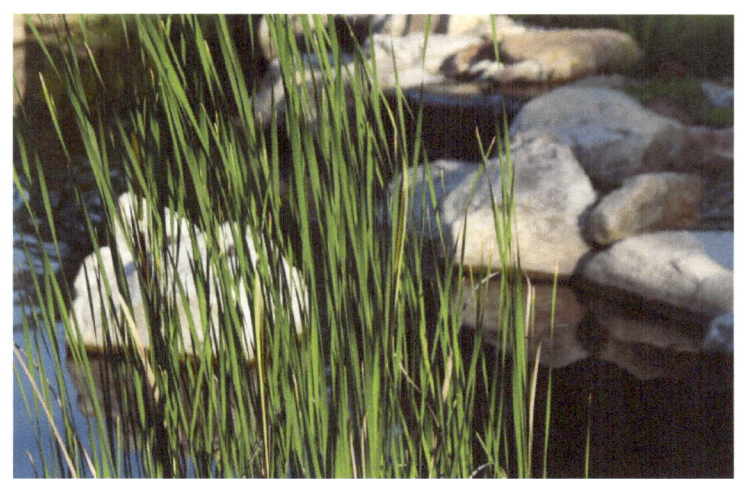

Grass Growing in Pond with Stone Edge

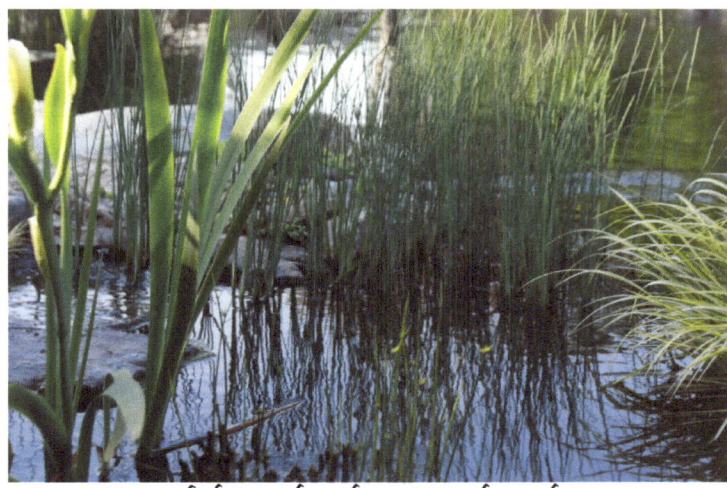

Peaceful Pond with Cat Tails and Grass

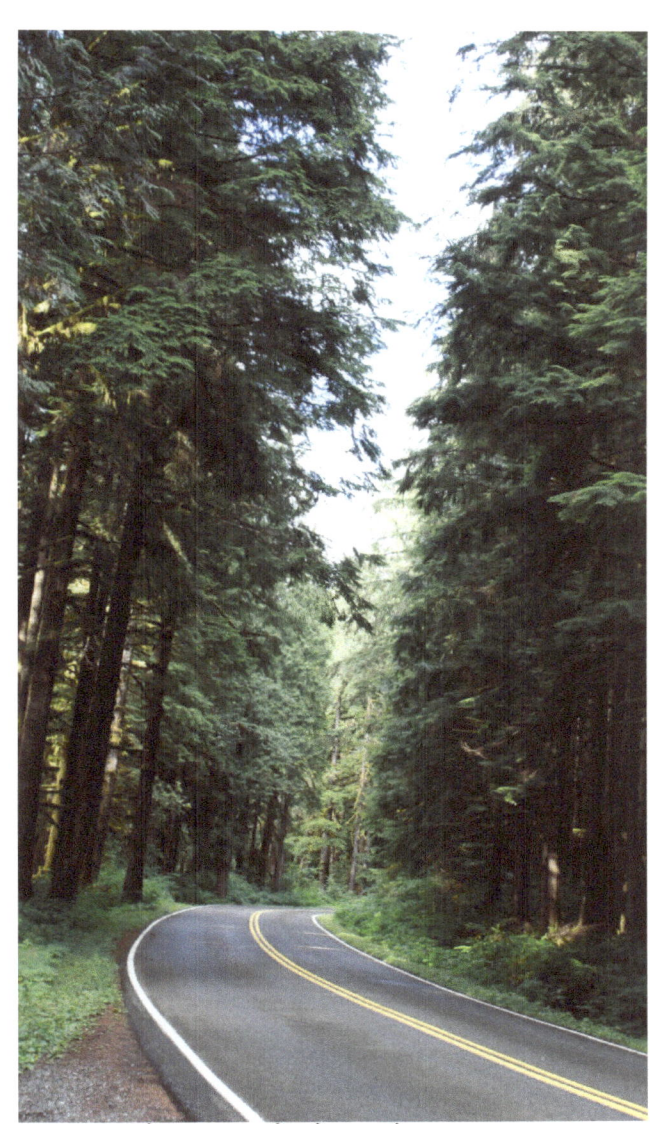

Winding Road Through Forrest

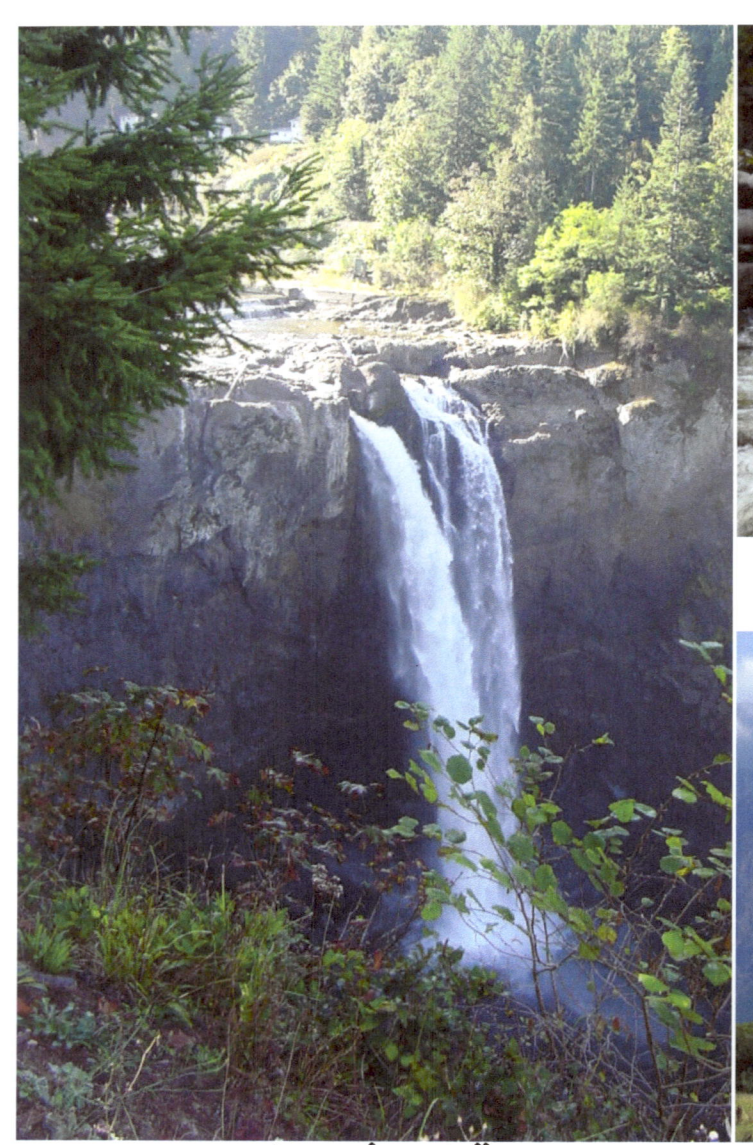

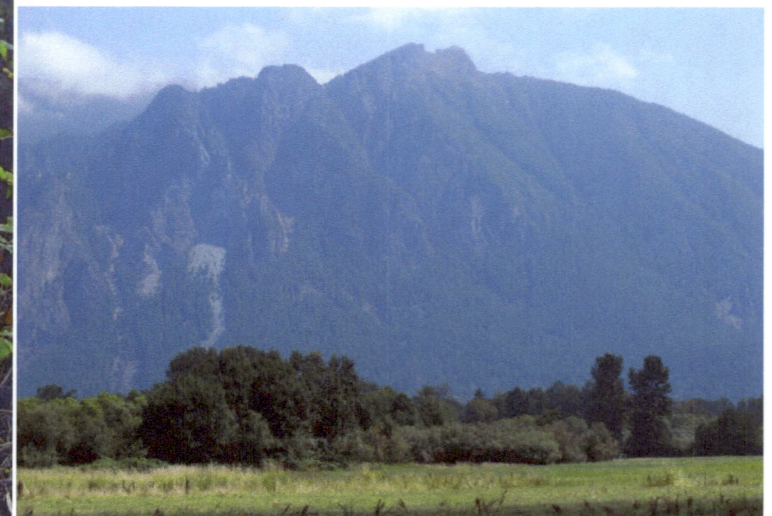

Cool Running Stream Waters

Snoqualmie Falls

View of Mount Si from Fall City, Washington

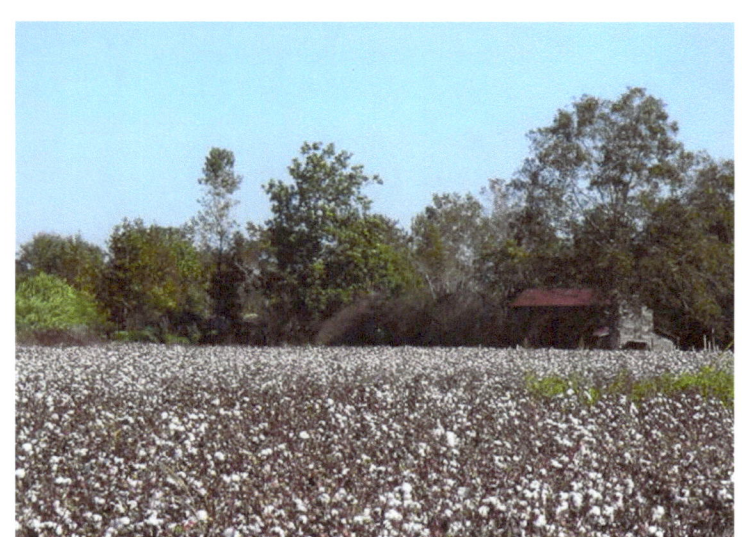

Rare Cotton Field Teachey, North Carolina

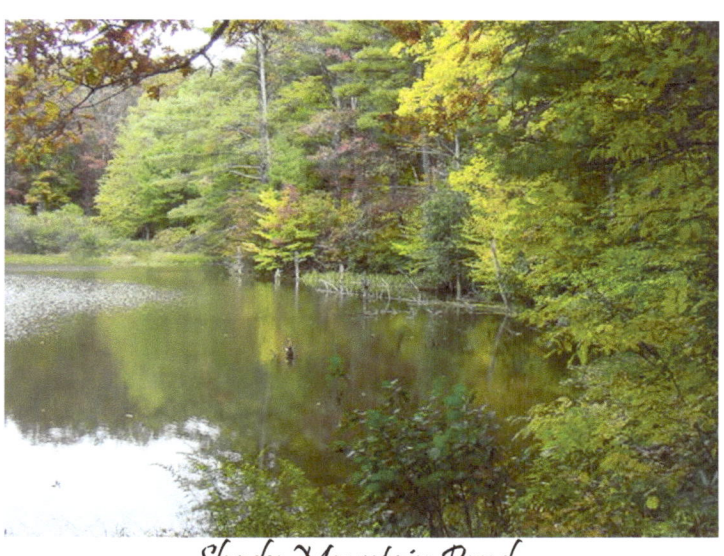

Shady Mountain Pond

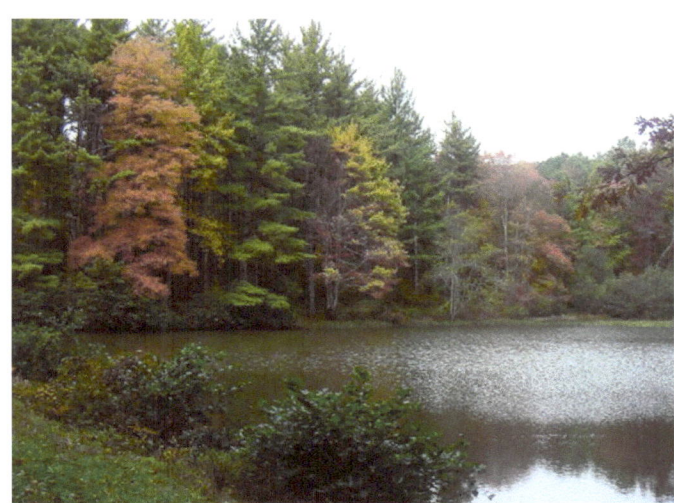

Mountain Pond in the Fall

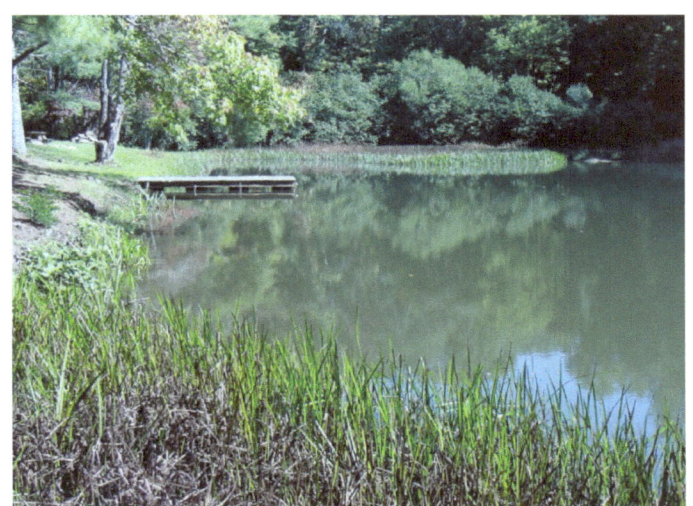

Summer Dock on Mountain Pond

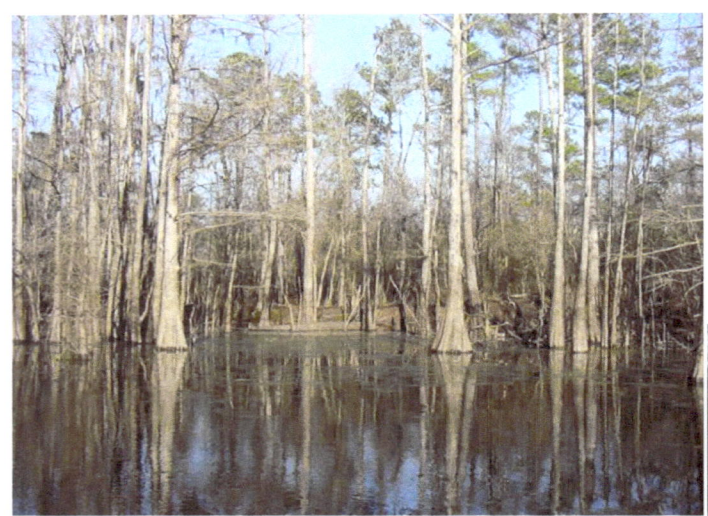

Pond Created by Beavers

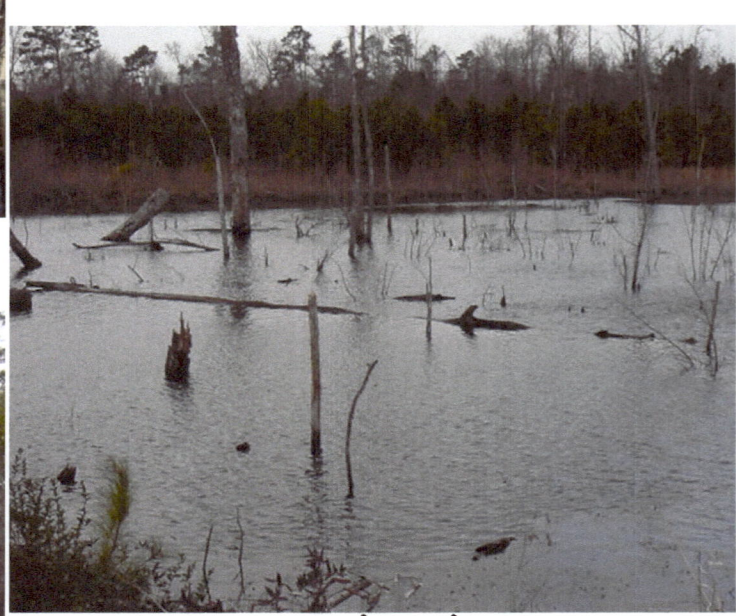

Duck Pond

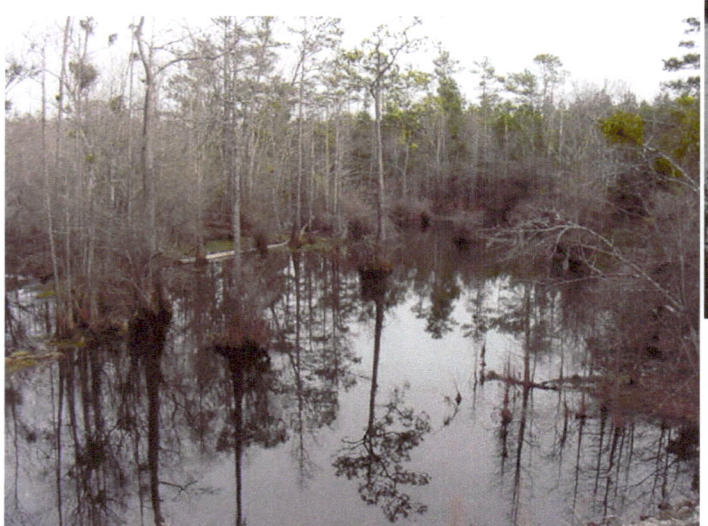

Cypress Trees in The Northeast Cape Fear River

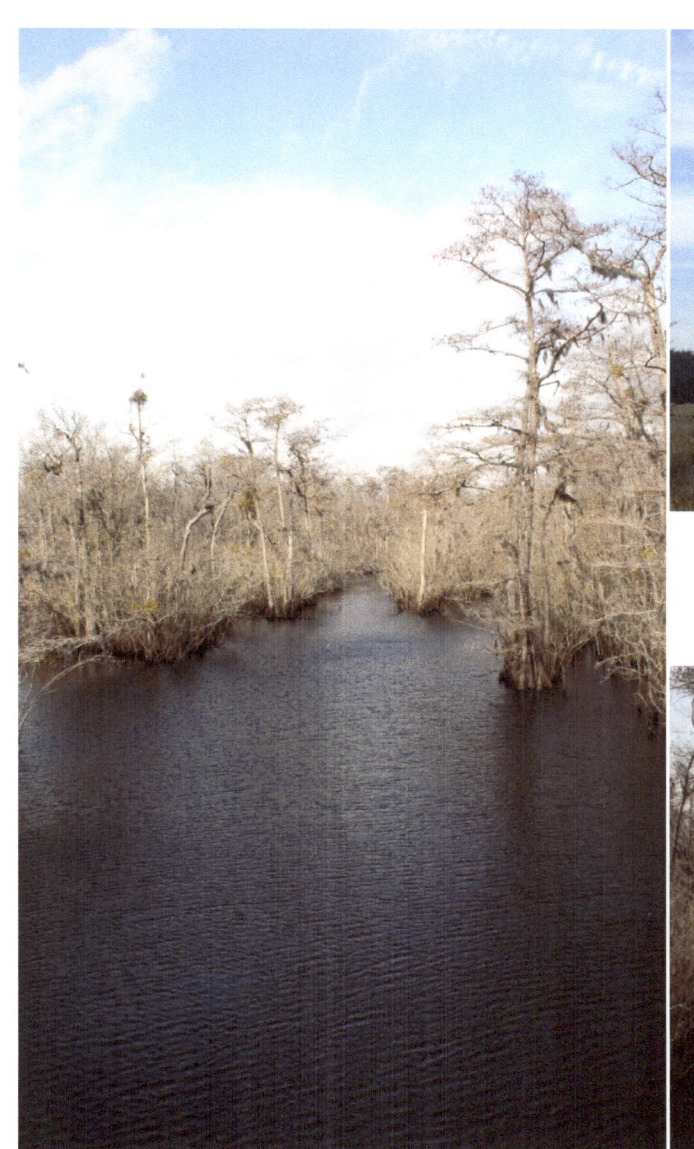

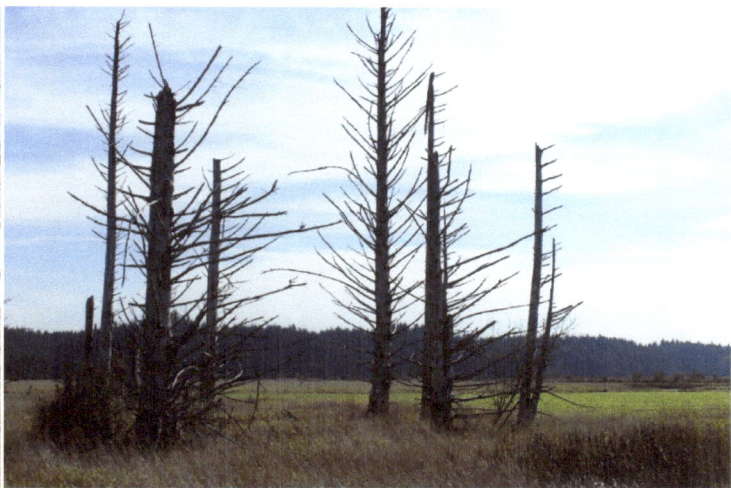

Land Near West Port, Washington

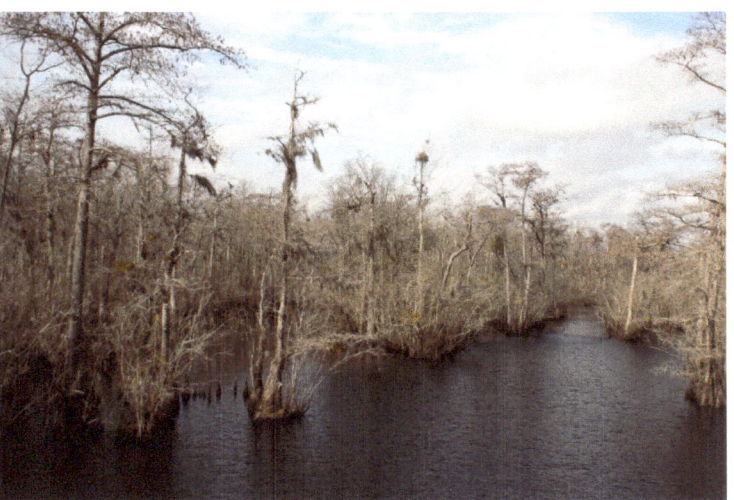

Cypress in the Black River

Black River Channel

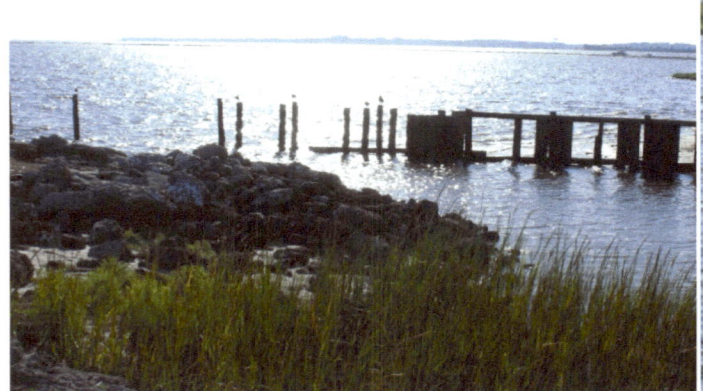

Dock at Fort Fisher

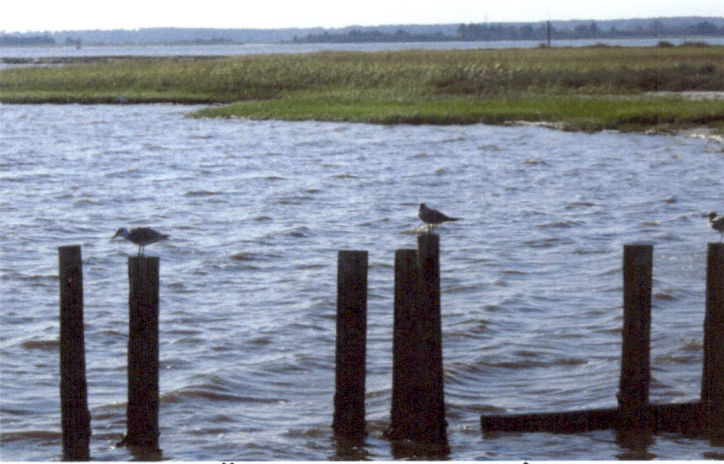

Gulls on Posts at Fort Fisher

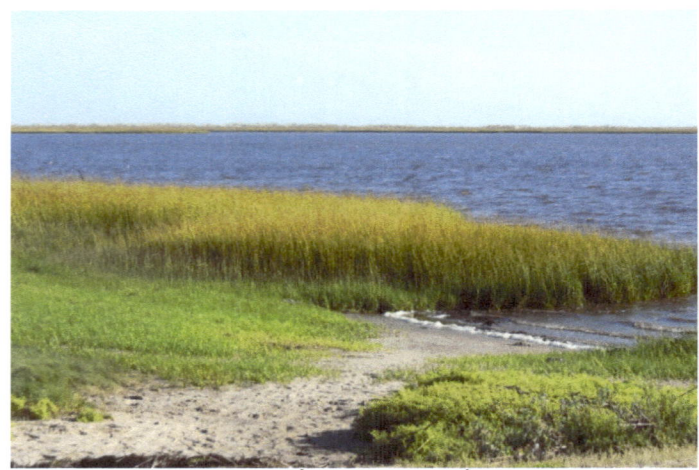

Sound at Fort Fisher

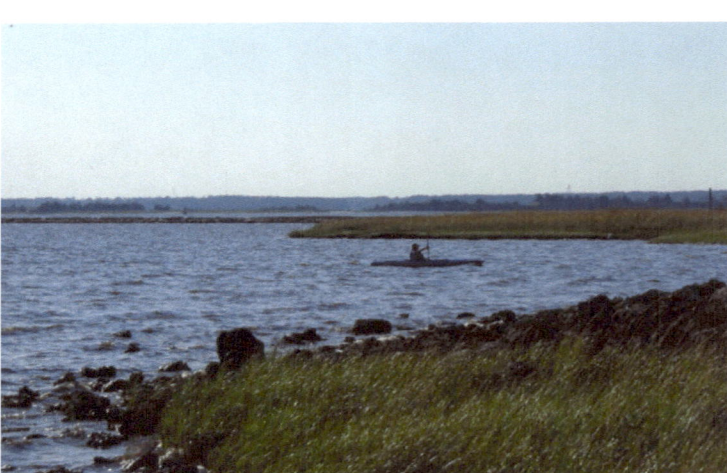

Kayaker at Fort Fisher

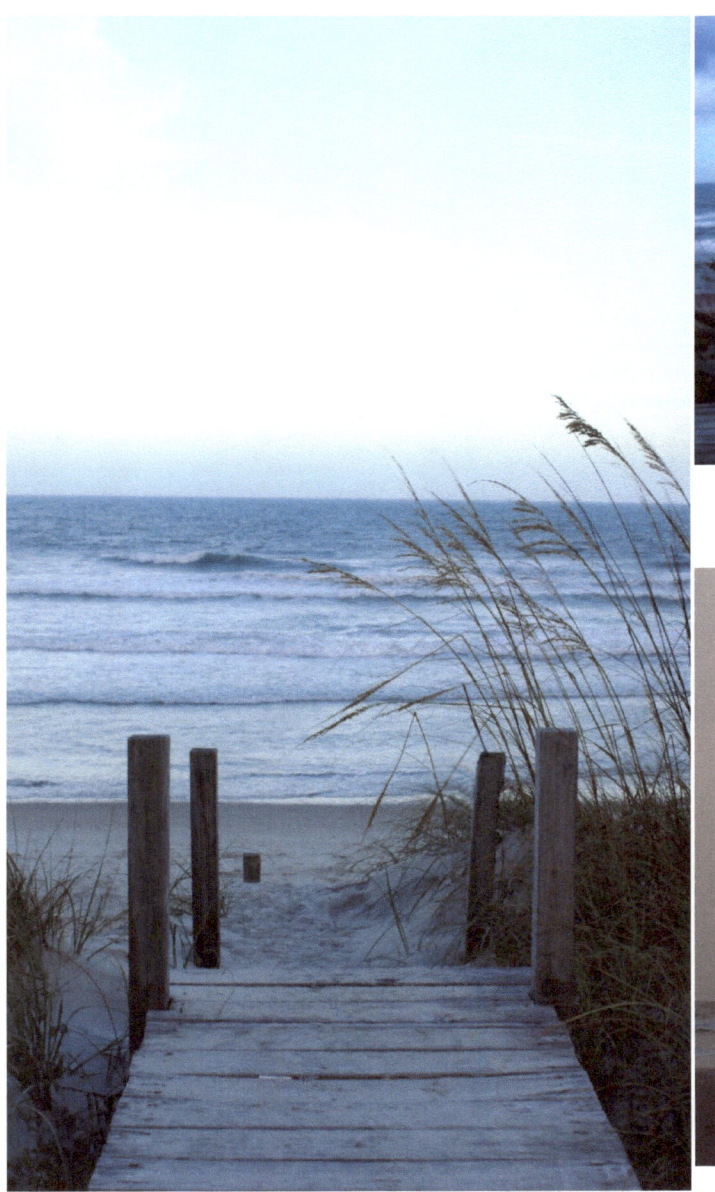

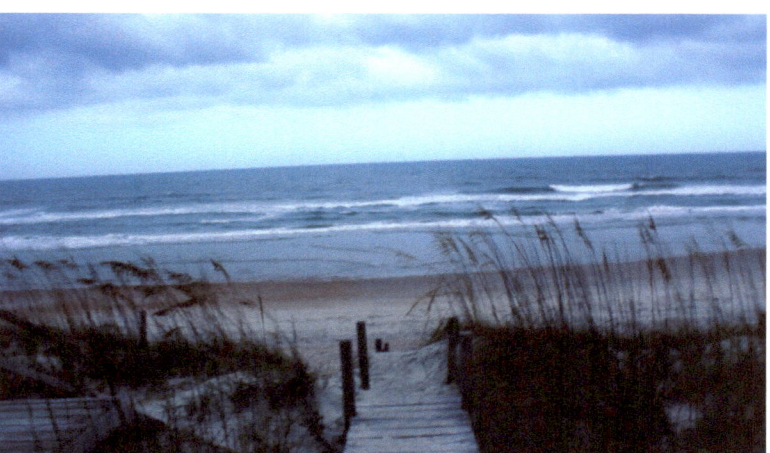

Early Morning Trip to Beach

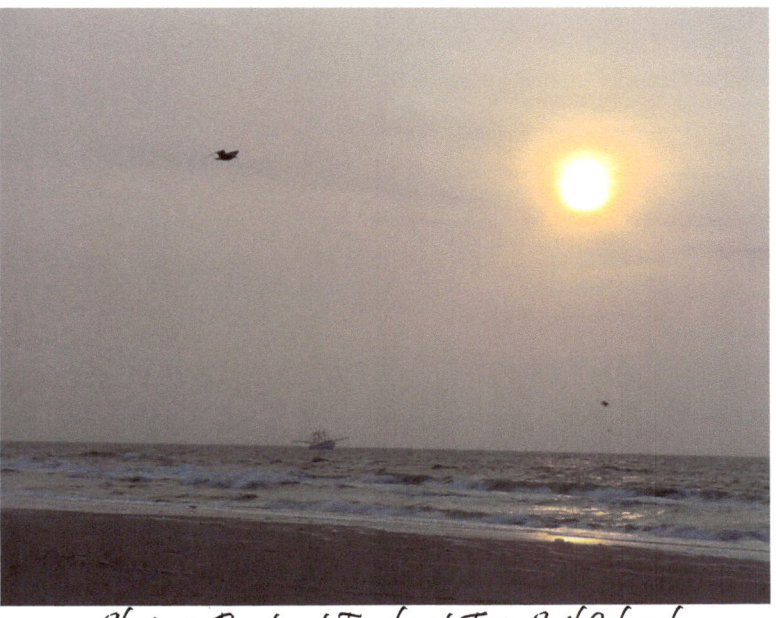

Beach Path at Top Sail Island

Shrimp Boat out Early at Top Sail Island

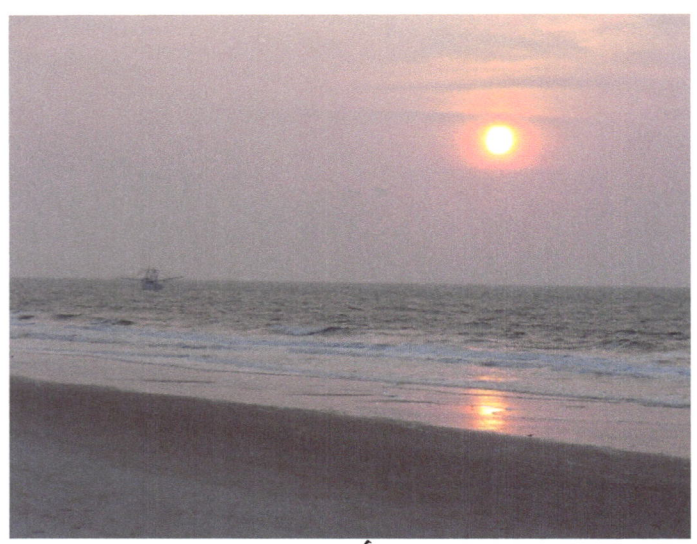

Sunrise Shrimpers

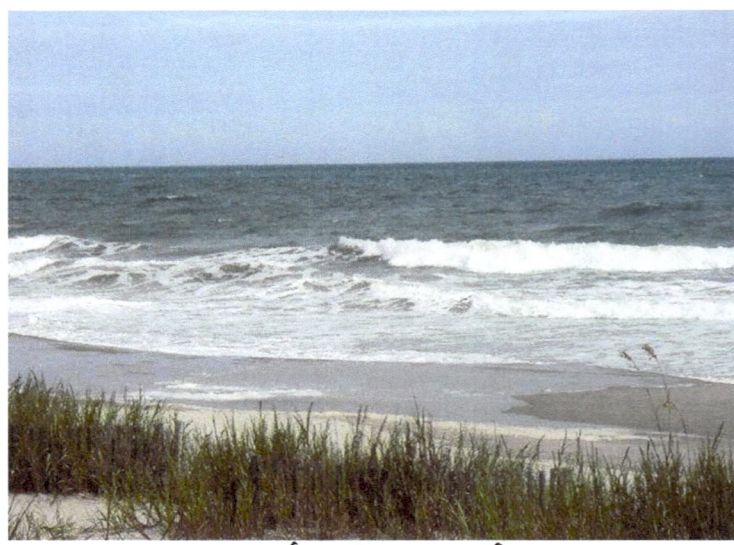

Carolina Ocean Surf

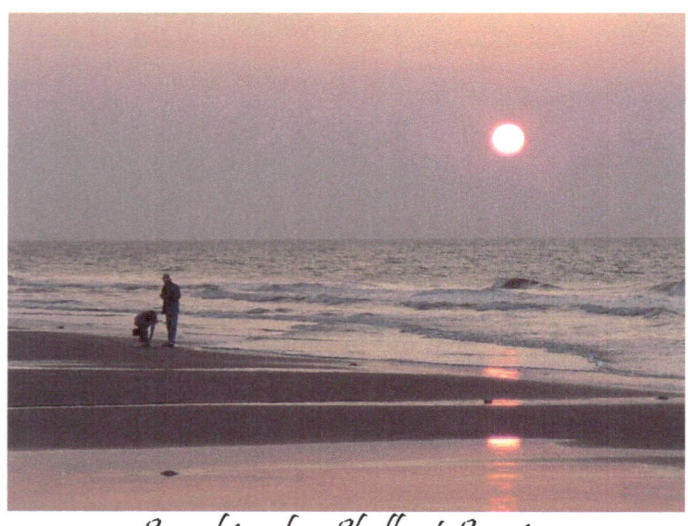

Searching for Shells at Sunrise

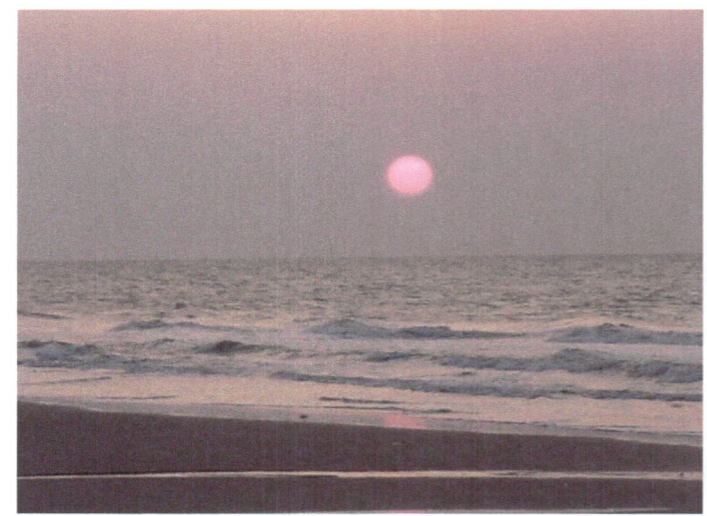

Sunrise

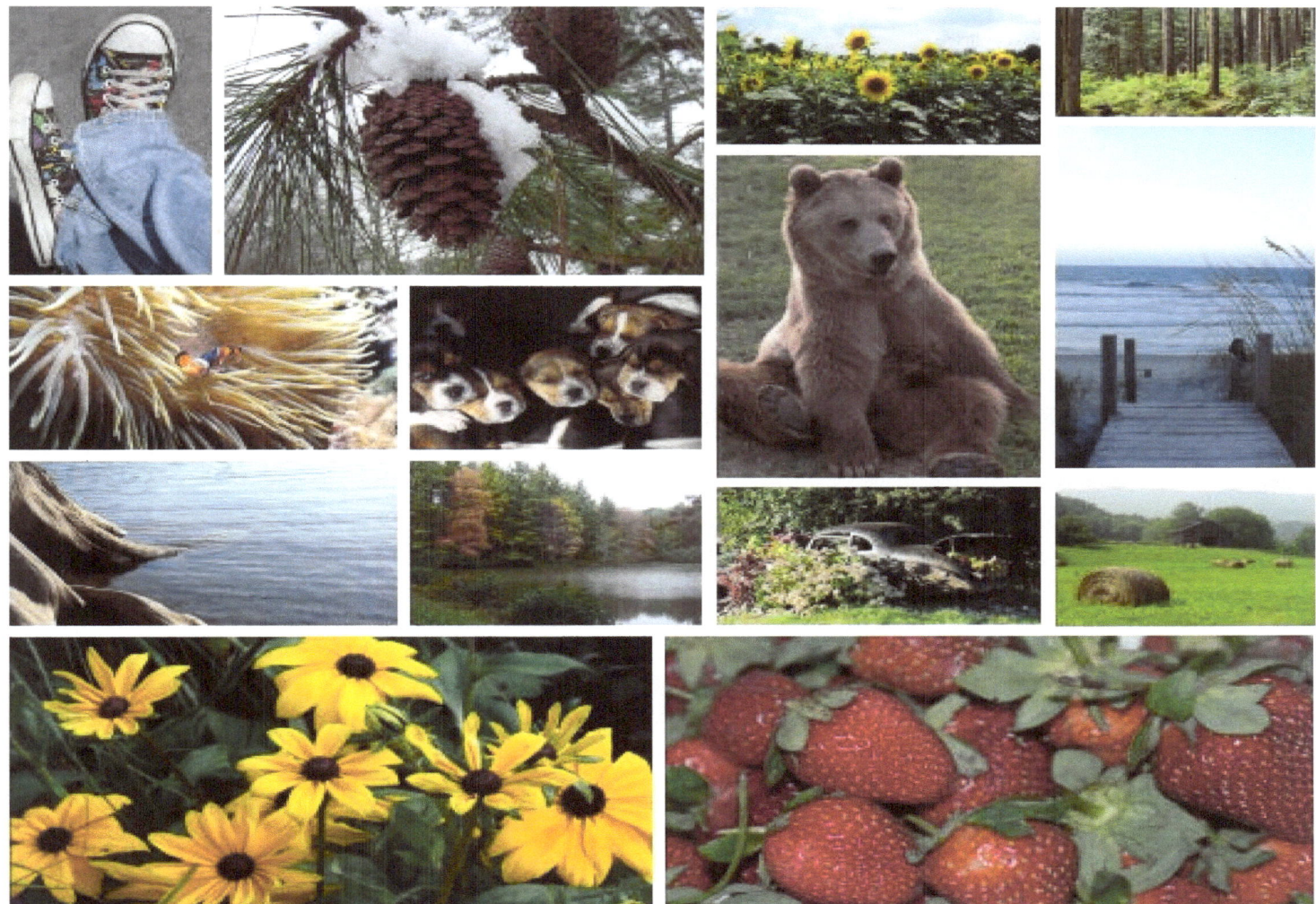